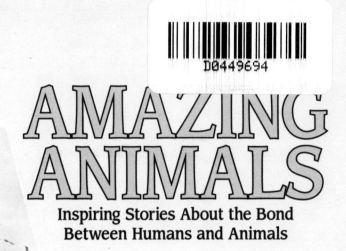

AMAZING ANIMALS

Inspiring Stories About the Bond Between Humans and Animals

AMAZING ANIMALS

Inspiring Stories About the Bond Between Humans and Animals

Janice Ryan

FOLK LORE PUBLISHING

© 2009 by Folklore Publishing
First printed in 2009 10 9 8 7 6 5 4 3 2 1
Printed in Canada

The Publisher: Folklore Publishing
Website: www.folklorepublishing.com

Library and Archives Canada Cataloguing in Publication

Ryan, Janice, 1954–

  Amazing animals: Inspiring Stories About the Bond Between Humans & Animals / by Janice Ryan.

Includes bibliographical references.
ISBN 978-1-894864-77-0

  1. Animals—Miscellanea. 2. Human-animal relationships—Miscellanea. I. Title.

QL50.R93 2009   590   C2009-900198-5

Project Director: Faye Boer
Project Editor: Wendy Pirk
Cover Image: Al Oeming Archives
Photo Credits: Photography credits: Every effort has been made to accurately credit the sources of photographs. Any errors or emissions should be reported directly to the publisher for correction in future editions. All photographs courtesy of Janice Ryan except the following: BC SPCA (p. 28); Debbie Cantlon (p. 144); Brent Cooke (p. 285, 287); Gwen Fehr (p. 183, 185); Cheryl Feldstein (p. 42); Delia Gruninger (p. 88a, 88b); Dick Jackson (p. 50); Karvonen Films Ltd. (p. 214); Johanna Kerby (p. 153); Bruce Kohlhofer (p. 95); Lois Lee (p. 179); Jim MacQuarrie (p. 229); Stephanie May (p. 134); Al Oeming Archives (p. 77, 81); Mark Pesklewis (p. 122); Samantha's mom (p. 107); Linda Sautner (p. 188); Andi Sime (p. 253).

We acknowledge the support of the Alberta Foundation for the Arts for our publishing program.
We acknowledge the financial support of the Government of Canada through the Book Publishing Industry Development Program (BPIDP) for our publishing activities.

 Canadian Heritage   Patrimoine canadien

Contents

Dedication

In loving memory of Gom, who opened her heart
and home to any animal in need, and to Duke,
my childhood best friend.

Acknowledgements

What a marvelous time I have had connecting with animal appreciators from around the globe. I feel as though I have made dozens of new friends.

To all of you storytellers who shared your remarkable tales and entrusted me to craft your stories with as much passion and sincerity as they were told, I thank you with heartfelt gratitude for opening your hearts and allowing me to jiggle your memories.

Special thanks to the Edmonton Valley Zoo, Wildlife Rehabilitation Society of Edmonton, Second Chance Animal Rescue Society, Todd Oeming, Nancy Stannard, and to Mark Pesklewis for photographing beautiful Lucy.

Thank you Larry Hendrick for helping me to find my footing and first words, and then cheering me on to the finish line.

A big thanks to my mom, Fay Viloski, for sharing stories about my great-grandma and grandmother and the menagerie of critters they lived with. Hugs to my animal-loving friends—Richard Gishler, Laurie Anfindsen, Carole Eder, Barbara Dunnett, Susan Turner—I appreciated every email and the articles you kindly clipped.

A big hug to Wendy Pirk for her keen editorial eye. To my dear friend and publisher, Faye Boer, thank you for listening to me enthusiastically gush anecdotes of kangaroos and chimps, until your eyes visibly glazed over. You never once told me to zip it, even though you wanted to.

And an enormous thank you to Dan, for preparing all those fabulous meals as the computer and I became one. Your mantra—"just keep writing"—worked. The tome is done.

Introduction

MOST OF US HAVE, at one time or another, had a strong emotional connection with an animal. Usually this love affair begins with a pet, our affections often won by a dog, a cat or a bird; sometimes, a horse or a hamster; perhaps a fish or a reptile. These pets become friends and members of the family; experiences are shared and bonds are forged. Our fellow earthlings seem to help us live a better, kinder life and, often, make us feel a little less alone as we wander, and occasionally stumble, through life.

Anyone who has spent time around animals will tell you flat out that these creatures have feelings, emotions, intelligence, a sense of humor and their own unique way of communicating. It seems that they are more like us and we are more like them than we ever could have imagined.

Animal life has always been a big part of my life. It has been the focus of my education, career choices and travels. When I gaze deeply into the eyes of an animal, I wonder, "What is going on in your head? What are you thinking and feeling today...at this moment?"

We are stewards of the earth, and the animals we share the planet with are in their own right amazing, magical beings. They possess abilities and instincts that often supersede humankind's powers and leave us in awe. Many of us, myself included, believe that animals are sentient beings. However, scientists will likely argue a good deal longer as to whether animals are capable of emotional lives. Humankind will certainly have a lot to reconsider if they deem the answer to be yes.

Nevertheless, I love science and studied four years to earn a science degree so that I could work as a biologist. But I am also a believer in observational and experiential conclusions. Not all things can be proven with experiments. Sometimes science doesn't tell the whole story. There is just no way to gather the facts and prove that something is or is not. You must believe what you see and accept what you experience. Surrender to the mysteries of nature, even if they elude understanding and scientific validation.

What a thrilling journey it has been writing *Amazing Animals*—I have spoken with people from all corners of the world, listening as they shared their personal encounters with the animal kingdom. From one passionate bird lover, I received a 64-page, handwritten letter describing the lives of various wild birds she and her husband have rescued and rehabilitated over the last 13 years. Was I surprised to get a 64-page letter? Not really, because that's the way animal lovers are. The lives of animals matter deeply, and the opportunity for people to share their story for others to enjoy and be inspired is part of the gratification.

The stories I have gathered show how utterly amazing animals are. They are tales of compassion and even empathy, heroism, intelligence, companionship, bonding and humor. Stories that no scientific doctrine could quantify or prove with an experiment, yet are nonetheless real. In some cases, the animal encounter was pivotal—a transformational experience that changed and, in some cases, *saved* a life.

These tales prove that we are not so very different from other animals, and it is this kinship that connects us to the natural world. So sit back, put your feet up and get ready to be amused, enlightened and charmed by these true stories of amazing animals.

~❊~

Section One
What a Pleasant Surprise

I am in favor of animal rights as well as human rights. That is the way of a whole human being.

—Abraham Lincoln

We share this earth with the rest of the natural world. The connection and kinship we have with other animal members links us all together. Life is, after all, about relationships: the relationships we forge with people and animals. And through these relationships, we get to know who we are.

I heard a story many years ago that conveyed a deep and moving message. The story was originally published in *The Star Thrower* by Loren Eiseley and has been rewritten and printed many times. Here is my adaptation:

One day a man was strolling along the beach when he noticed a boy picking something up and gently tossing it into the ocean.

He approached the lad and asked, "What are you doing?"

The boy replied, "I'm saving the starfish. The tide is going out and if I don't throw them back, they'll die."

The man said, "There are miles of beaches and hundreds of starfish. What difference does it make?"

The boy listened and bent down to pick up another starfish. As he threw it into the surf he replied with a smile, "It made a difference to that one."

CHAPTER ONE

Guardian Angels

The soul is the same in all living creatures, although the body of each is different.

—Hippocrates

ALTHOUGH NO ANIMAL HAS ever asked to go to war, many have indeed served. They have worked hard and given their lives, often in an effort to save the lives of humans. Through the ages, these animals have been honored for their bravery.

But every now and then, an animal makes headlines for saving a human life in situations that are closer to home: "Dog Finds Buried Skier Alive" or "Pig Saves Family From Fire" are a couple of true examples. One of my favorites is from a headline published in the *New York Times* on May 8, 1903. It reads: "Parrot Saves Master's Life. Man Was Bleeding to Death When the Bird's Screams for Help Brought Aid."

Even in 1903, people were interested in and encouraged by these heartwarming tales. It's good to know there are animal angels—pawed, clawed and finned—that are looking out for us...even when we least expect it.

Gorilla Mother Rescues Boy

Scientists have known for a long time that nonhuman primates, such as gorillas and chimpanzees, share upward of 97.7 percent of our DNA. Like us, our closest relatives possess a large brain, the intelligence to learn and pass on information and the ability to make and use tools.

Although humans have the most sophisticated language, even that boundary has been blurred. Koko, the world's most famous gorilla, communicates with humans by using American Sign Language. She understands and uses more than 1000 words of sign language, and understands more than 2000 words of spoken English. Imagine looking into the eyes of a great ape and exchanging thoughts and feelings. Wow!

The late Dian Fossey opened the world's eyes to the extraordinary lives and behaviors of gorillas. She devoted her life to understanding these animals and was on a fervent quest to protect them from poaching. Her campaign was very public, and she was murdered in Africa, likely as a result of her outspoken views.

Another primate expert, Jane Goodall, continues to dedicate her life to studying chimpanzees, encouraging the world to help save the dwindling populations and urging scientists to find other means of gathering research than allowing these intelligent animals to suffer in labs. Both women helped to narrow the gap between our perception of ourselves and primates.

The more we learn about these animals, the more our differences shrink. Charles Darwin argued in *The Descent of Man* (published in 1871) that any animal endowed with social instincts—the skill and need to act together with others—"would inevitably acquire a moral sense or conscience, as soon as its intellectual powers had become as well, or nearly as well developed, as in man."

Although not all people believe that animals have morals or a conscience, the possibility was certainly on everyone's minds at the Brookfield Zoo's gorilla exhibit on August 16, 1996. No witnesses will ever forget the scene that day in Chicago, Illinois. The memory will likely surface often as the debate about the "missing link" between humans and the great apes continues.

On that day, visitors gathered around the bamboo fence encircling the gorilla exhibit and watched in horror as a three-year-old boy ran up to the fence and inadvertently flipped over the top, falling 24 feet into the enclosure. The boy lay unconscious in the pit as several western lowland gorillas scurried around, curious about their sudden visitor.

The boy's mother was panic-stricken as her son lay unmoving among the great apes. Zoo attendants acted immediately, but before they could remove the child, an eight-year-old female named Binti Jua reached the boy.

Onlookers had no idea what to expect; as the gorilla approached the boy, the mood grew even more anxious. Gorillas are large and strong. The females normally weigh between 180 and 200 pounds, and the males can be up to 425 pounds. Though Binti Jua was smaller than the other four females, weighing only 165 pounds, her stature was just as imposing.

What happened next was truly remarkable. Binti Jua moved her baby, Koola, from her arms to her back. Then she stooped down and gently lifted the boy into her arms. She seemed to sense that the boy was injured, and when another female gorilla advanced their way, Binti Jua turned her back as if to shield the boy. The silverback male was not on display that day, which was fortunate because he may have interpreted the unexpected visitor as a threat.

Binti Jua carefully cradled the boy in her muscular, hairy arms. She herself was a relatively new first-time mom, and she handled him as she did her own gorilla baby.

The boy's head was nestled in her left arm as her right arm supported his body and legs. The gorilla looked up with concern and bewilderment as the crowd gazed down on her with amazement, the whole while gently patting the little boy's bottom with her right hand, just as a human would do to reassure a little one that everything was all right.

By now, zoo staff members had been alerted and were directing the gorillas to their off-exhibit holding area. Using three water hoses pointed at the floor, they signaled the gorillas to go to the doors leading to their overnight quarters.

Binti Jua used a separate door from the other females. The staff had taught her to bring them her baby for periodic examinations. So, as trained, Binti Jua walked 60 feet toward her assigned door, carrying the little boy with her. But instead of going through the door into her holding area, she gently set the boy down outside the entrance. Then, with her baby still clinging to her back, she joined the other gorillas and entered *their* holding area.

The staff was astonished: Binti Jua delivered the child to them just as she had done many times before with her own baby. The boy was whisked to the hospital. He spent four days under care and, thankfully, made a full recovery.

Coincidently, Binti Jua is the niece of Koko, the famous "signing" gorilla. She was hand raised by staff at the San Francisco Zoo and was later transferred to the Brookfield Zoo for lessons in mothering, in preparation for her own baby's birth. Hand-reared animals often lack nurturing skills they would have obtained in the wild and need to be trained for motherhood by observing others of their kind. Binti Jua must have been a model pupil.

The incident was recounted on The Gorilla Foundation website, an organization dedicated to the preservation, protection and well-being of gorillas. The foundation is where Dr. Penny Patterson works with Koko in the field of interspecies communication. Her discoveries over the years have changed perceptions about gorilla intelligence.

Dr. Patterson wrote, "Although Binti's maternal instinct might lead her to pick up the child, her intelligence was demonstrated when she moved the child to the human access door."

As primatologists have observed, this display of caring behavior is common among female gorillas. Binti Jua's maternal instincts provided concern and empathy for this injured child just as gorillas have been know to show sick or injured members of their family and troop. Her actions helped prove that a gentle spirit exists in gorillas and dispel the myth that they are fierce, heartless animals.

A zoo visitor captured the entire episode on video, and the footage circulated the globe, making headline news. Binti Jua was hailed a hero—an international sensation. *The Oprah Winfrey Show* covered the story, and *Newsweek Magazine* named her "Hero of the Year" a few months later.

Whether out of a sense of moral duty or because of her training, this great ape acted in a tender, responsible way and safely delivered the boy to her keepers. Binti showed only concern for a child who had accidentally fallen into her domain. On that day, the spirit of Binti Jua, which means "daughter of sunshine" in Swahili, shone brightly.

Creature Feature

Gorillas live in family groups called troops, consisting of two to 20 individuals. The silver-back male, named for the wide saddle of silver fur across his back, is the only adult male in the troop; the others are adult females and their offspring. The silverback has the huge responsibility of protecting the troop.

A Hopping Hero

The noble kangaroo is one of Australia's iconic and beloved symbols. *Skippy the Bush Kangaroo*, a popular children's television series produced in the late '60s in Australia, immortalized the kangaroo. This unique animal became a familiar face in living rooms around the world.

Kangaroos appear to be a combination of several animals: they have a small deer-like head and a pear-shaped body with a large bottom, they stand upright on two hind legs like a human, and they are the only large animals to hop like a frog. And to really confuse the issue, females often appear as if they have two heads, one on top of their necks and the other poking out from the middle of their tummy. The smaller noggin, of course, belongs to the baby or joey, snugly nestled in its mama's pouch.

An estimated 25 million kangaroos bounce across the landscape of the "land down under" and though "kangaroo crossing" signs are a common sight along Australian highways, bright lights and engine noise can startle the animal, causing it to leap in front of a car. A joey can live up to five days in the pouch of its dead mother, so rescue organizations remind people that if they find a dead kangaroo or wallaby to always check in the pouch in case there is a joey alive inside.

In 2000, the Richards family rescued a tiny eastern grey kangaroo baby after its mother was killed by a car. The infant was gently removed from the pouch and taken home to be hand raised. Young kangaroos are normally kept in the pouch until they are about nine months old, but they continue to be suckled until about 18 months of age.

The Richards named the joey Lulu, and the entire family—Len, Lynn and their children Luke and Celeste—helped raise the baby "roo." In no time, Lulu became a valued member of the family and was even accepted by the cat and dog.

As Lulu grew, she roamed freely around the Richards' property and the surrounding bush land, grazing on grass, leaves and bark. She also enjoyed family time with the Richards, coming inside for a visit to get a cuddle or a treat, or gathering around the fire with the family on cooler nights.

Lulu bonded with the family, especially Len, and she waited for him to come home at the end of the workday. She followed him around the property as he made his rounds on their ranch in the Gippsland region of Victoria state, in southeast Australia.

In September 2003, Len went out to investigate the property for damage after a severe storm had hit the area. Lulu accompanied him as he wandered about, checking things out. During the walk, a large tree branch fell, striking the 52-year-old man on the head and knocking him unconscious.

Lulu responded by standing guard over Len's motionless body and making an unusual croaking sound. "She was obviously trying to get our attention because she never acts like that," 17-year-old Celeste Richards told the Associated Press.

"It went on for about 15 minutes, so we went outside to investigate and saw Lulu standing upright with her chest puffed out over Dad's body. If it wasn't for her, my dad could have died. Lulu is my hero."

Without the help of Lulu's persistent alarm call, the Richards family would not have found Len so quickly. A rural ambulance was called to pick him up, and he was flown by air ambulance to Melbourne for treatment.

CNN reported that Len had told the Australian Broadcasting Corporation radio that Lulu also appeared to have applied some first aid: "My nephew, when he got to my side, said she'd actually tipped me on my side, and vomit was coming out of my mouth, so she'd actually saved me from choking."

It seems that Lulu used the same quick thinking as Skippy, the ingenious hero of the famed television series. Skippy alerted his human pal, Sonny, whenever anyone got into trouble in the outback. Maybe Lulu caught an episode or two because her actions helped save the life of her owner and mate, Len Richards.

On May 19, 2004, Lulu was honored with the Royal Society for the Prevention of Cruelty to Animals "National Animal Valor Award," the country's highest award presented for heroic animal deeds. Lulu is the first kangaroo and the only indigenous animal ever to receive this rare and prestigious award.

It would seem that in Lulu's books, one good turn deserves another: four years earlier, Len Richards and his family had saved Lulu's life, and now Lulu saved Len's life. The circle is complete, and this resourceful kangaroo certainly earned her title as a hero.

Len sent a note in May 2009 saying: "Lulu is still here coming home on regular basis for her cuddle, treat and warmth around the fire. She has even brought a couple of her friends home with her on different occasions."

Creature Feature

The red kangaroo, standing six feet tall and weighing 300 pounds, is the largest kangaroo species. It can hop over 40 miles per hour and leap distances of 25 feet and heights of 10 feet. Adult males are known as bucks, boomers or jacks; females are called flyers or does. Kangaroos live together in groups called mobs.

Jarod, My Hero!

It was early evening in the last week of September 2007. The crisp scent of fall was in the air, and it was just starting to get dark. Donna Perreault was at home with her two chow chows in the tiny community of Genelle, located in southern British Columbia.

Donna was on the phone talking to her son in Texas while Jarod, her black male chow, was curled up nearby and Meesha, the red-haired female, was enjoying a snooze outside next to the truck. All of a sudden, Donna heard a deep guttural bark—Meesha's "serious" voice. Donna glanced through the window in time to see a black bear running full speed toward her dog. Donna dropped the phone in a panic and ran out the door yelling as loudly as she could. All she could think about was the safety of her beloved dog.

Bears are a fairly regular occurrence in this area. The town is nestled along the bank of the Columbia River and is surrounded by rolling hillsides, open terrain, rivers and the Kootenay Rockies. It is the perfect setting for nature lovers in search of scenery and wildlife and, of course, it's a wonderful place to live if you are a bear. Bears are normally not a concern for Donna or the locals; the town's motto is "give them their space and enjoy their grandeur." Apparently this bear, while out for an evening stroll, had one thing on his mind, namely Donna's dog Meesha.

Donna's yelling startled the bear. He got off Meesha and ran around to the back of the truck. Meesha was almost 12 years old and was showing her age, but she decided to defend her territory and started after him. As the bear turned to attack, Jarod came bounding around the truck, much to Donna's surprise and dismay. She thought he was safely tucked away inside the house, but the door must not have latched as she ran outside.

Now Jarod was involved in the fight. The six-year-old dog jumped at the bear with force and focused determination. The bear alternated between charging and swiping at Jarod, then turning to shake and bite Meesha. Donna noticed a bucket, broom and shovel near the door. She picked up the bucket and threw it at the bear.

The bear's attention was now directed toward Donna. He swatted at her chest, leaving a nasty gash. As she tried to back away, Jarod continued biting and attacking the bear, but the bear's focus was back on Donna. She grabbed the mop, and swinging it with all her might, smacked him across the snout.

The bear stopped for a beat before turning on Donna for the third time. Jarod was not about to let this bruin kill his devoted owner *or* his canine companion. He assaulted the bear with increasing ferocity, repeatedly sinking his teeth into the animal's hide. The bear took the bait and shifted his attention away from Meesha and Donna to Jarod. The chow ran away from the truck, darting behind the garage with the bear in close pursuit.

Donna could now focus on Meesha. The elderly chow had been thrown around a lot, and she was soaked with bear saliva. Meesha wanted to go after the bear as well, so Donna took hold of her collar and ushered her into the house out of harm's way before spinning around to search for Jarod.

Donna anxiously called out his name. When Jarod's head poked around the corner of the garage, Donna was making her way to the shovel, just in case. Jarod, to her great relief, was alone. Says Donna, "We both ran into the house, and I shut the door."

Then she remembered her son on the other end of the phone. She could hear him yelling, "Mom, Mom!" He had actually been able to hear much of the commotion outside through the open window. His mother's screams and a cacophony of growling and barking had traveled the airwaves. He asked if she was okay, and only then did she remember that the bear's claw had slashed her. In the adrenalin rush, it had slipped her mind.

"I looked down and saw my torn shirt. I had a wound that looked like it had been sliced with a filet knife." There were other claw marks and punctures as well, but Donna insists the tetanus shot she later received hurt more than her wounds.

Now it was time to check the dogs. There had been a full-out war between the bear and her pooches; she was not sure what she would find. "To my amazement," Donna recalls, "there was only one shallow mark on Jarod's back. Meesha was covered in saliva around her neck fur, but no puncture wounds. Incredible!" Meesha needed some chiropractic adjustments on her back, but she was in one piece.

Jarod's act of heroism earned him two prestigious honors: he received the British Columbia SPCA's 2008 Animal Hero Award and in 2009, he was inducted into the Purina Animal Hall of Fame, which has recognized hero animals from across Canada for 41 years.

He risked his life to defend both Donna and Meesha from serious harm, possibly even death.

Donna proudly shows off Jarod's Animal Hero Award.

❧❦❧

"I can't even begin to tell you how much we love and appreciate Jarod. He is such a brave, devoted companion."

Donna adopted Jarod when he was four years old, after learning that he was about to be euthanized. The Northwest Chow Rescue in Oregon was urgently searching for a home for him. Donna's sister says, "You saved Jarod's life when you adopted him, and he saved yours and Meesha's life."

In Donna's eyes, Jarod was already a godsend. Now, he is also her hero.

Finned Lifeguards

There had been only nine shark attacks in California's Monterey County waters since 1952, so being attacked by a great white shark was the last thing on Todd Endris' mind as he paddled through the water the morning of August 28, 2007, to enjoy the sport he loves most—surfing. It was like any other day of surfing—Todd and his pals were out on the water catching waves at Marina State Beach.

Todd had only been in the water for about 15 minutes when out of nowhere came a shark. Todd told *The Today Show*, "There's no warning at all. Maybe I saw him a quarter second before it hit me—but no warning. It was just a giant shark. It just shows you what a perfect predator they really are."

He was sitting on his surfboard when a 17-foot-long, 3000-pound shark slammed into the front of the board. The shark's gaping jaws were enormous, but it was not able to grab both Todd and his board.

The shark hit a second time; Todd was lying on his surfboard, and the shark was able to clamp Todd's torso and board into his mouth like a sandwich. The razor-sharp teeth shredded the skin of Todd's back, but luckily his stomach was pressed against the board, protecting his intestines and vital organs.

In a third attack, the great white tried to swallow Todd's right leg. A tug-of-war ensued. The shark's grip actually anchored Todd and allowed him to fight back. He fiercely kicked the fish in the head and snout with his left leg until it finally let him go. Todd's leg was mauled to the bone, but at least the 24-year-old man was alive.

Todd had fought the largest predatory fish on Earth with everything he had. According to Todd, "It's a fight-or-flight response. Everything is happening so fast. You have to fight."

A pod of bottlenose dolphins had been in the water all morning, playing in the surf, as dolphins like to do. Todd's surfing buddy Wes Williams was in the water near Todd and thought nothing of it when the dolphins swam by him and started circling Todd.

Wes was looking toward the shore when he heard Todd yell. He whipped his head around and saw that Todd had been knocked off his board and was hanging in the water. The dolphins were circling around him and thrashing. One dolphin even leapt out of the water and swung its tail around. In his account of the incident on Surfline, a surf-related website, Wes wrote that he wondered what Todd had done to "piss off the dolphins."

Then, Wes noticed blood oozing out into a large circle, and he realized there was a shark in the water. The dolphins had encircled Todd and were forcefully slapping the bloody water with their tails. Brian Simpson, another surfer pal, saw the dolphins ram the shark as they formed a barrier between Todd and the great white. A dolphin's snout is made of strong and thick bone, making it an effective and dangerous weapon.

The dolphins' arrival was the miracle Todd needed to get out of the situation alive. They kept the shark at a distance, allowing Todd the chance to climb back on his board and escape. Luck hit a second time when a wave rolled in. Todd was able to catch the wave and ride back to shore.

Brian Simpson, an off-duty X-ray technician, was already on the beach ready to help his severely injured friend. He administered life-saving first aid until the paramedics arrived on the scene. Todd had lost half of his blood. He was flown by helicopter to a nearby hospital for treatment. It took 500 stitches and 200 staples to close the wounds.

Without the protective intervention of the dolphins, Todd would likely never have made it back to shore. Once he was off his board and in the water, he was truly shark bait. As for the shark, it went on its merry way, free to come and go as it pleased inside the protected waters of the marine wildlife refuge. In Todd's eyes, this is the way it should be.

"I wouldn't want to go after the shark anyway," Todd said. "We're in his realm, not the other way around."

Todd would need many months of physical therapy to repair the muscle damage, but he did not want fear to get in the way of his love for surfing. Just six weeks after the incident, he mustered the courage to go back and surf the exact location of the terrifying attack.

Now, Todd is spearheading the International Shark Attack Research Fund advisory committee, which is dedicated to the understanding of the shark-human-dolphin dynamic in the hopes of preventing future shark attacks.

Dolphins have been known to use defensive behavior—ramming with their snouts, leaping in the air and smacking with their flippers and tails— to protect an injured or sick member of their pod from shark attacks. It seems they are only too happy to help scare off sharks during an attack on a human as well. These life-saving acts of kindness have been recorded all over the world.

Martin Richardson, from Colchester, England, was swimming in the Red Sea in 1996 when a shark attacked him. He suffered severe bites to several parts of his body, including one bite that slightly punctured his lung. Three bottlenose dolphins came to his rescue and encircled him, scaring off the shark. The dolphins saved his life.

In 2002, Grant Dickson's trawler sank off the coast of Queensland, Australia. Bleeding profusely, he clung to an upturned dinghy as a group of sharks circled him. One shark was moving in closer and closer when a pod of dolphins came on the scene and scared the sharks off. He told reporters that he owed his life to the dolphins.

No one can say for sure why dolphins seem to like humans, coming to their aid at the most unexpected times, but for Todd Endris and fellow land dwellers who find themselves in trouble at sea, having finned friends like these dolphins is akin to having an aquatic guardian angel.

CHAPTER TWO

Heaven Can Wait

*Life is as dear to the mute creature as it is to
a man. Just as one wants happiness and fears
pain, just as one wants to live and not to die,
so do other creatures.*

—the Dalai Lama

THE STORY OF NOAH, AS he boarded creatures two by
two onto his ark to save them from the flood, was
possibly the first recorded organized effort to
rescue animals.

The first animal protection society in the world
started up in London in 1824—the Royal Society
for the Prevention of Cruelty to Animals (RSPCA).
At that time, animals were generally regarded as
commodities for supplying food, transport and
sport. Showing animals compassion was regarded
as rather bizarre behavior.

In 1866, the American Society for the Prevention of Cruelty to Animals (ASPCA) opened in
New York, and nine days later it passed the first
anti-animal-cruelty law in the U.S. to protect farm

and work animals, primarily horses. The organization went on to successfully pass laws to include cats and dogs.

Today there are many dedicated, hard-working organizations whose sole purpose is to rescue and rehabilitate animals. As well, there are plenty of caring souls who act alone or rally the troops with a plan to help the lives of those who cannot speak for themselves.

On occasion, people's compassion and urgency to save an animal's life may overshadow their fear and logic; they will risk their own lives and safety to act on the deed. Their selfless actions are a gentle reminder that *all* life is valuable.

A Life Worth Saving

In April 2008, I attended a lecture on the environment and wildlife preservation given by Dr. Jane Goodall. She is undoubtedly the world's most celebrated primatologist, known for her ardent work and advocacy on behalf of chimpanzees. They are similar to humans, both genetically and physically, and because of their high intelligence, Dr. Goodall believes they can teach us a lot about other nonhuman primates.

She told a story of a man who, at great risk to his own personal safety, had saved the life of a drowning chimpanzee. Jane Goodall is an impassioned speaker, and I'm sure her words penetrated the hearts and imaginations of everyone in the auditorium. Her words were simple, but the strength of the message left the audience moved and introspective. I have not forgotten the feeling of awe that washed over me as she told this story, nor will I any time soon.

A chimpanzee named Jo-Jo was only a year and a half old when his mother was shot in Africa. The young chimp was shipped to a zoo in North America, where he languished for over a decade in a small cage with iron bars and a cement floor. This highly intelligent, social being was alone, cooped up and bored beyond belief. He was living a barren existence in solitary confinement, and he had done nothing wrong.

A new director at the Detroit Zoo decided to build the biggest exhibit in North America. He gathered a group of chimpanzees and designed an enclosure surrounded by a water-filled moat. Chimps don't know how to swim, so the idea was that the public would have good visual access to the chimps without the distraction of bars and mesh fences, and the chimps could not escape because they don't like water.

In the chimpanzee community, males compete for dominance with displays that involve bristling hair, vocalizations, throwing rocks and such. It is a typical part of their lives together. But on July 29, 1990, a routine display almost turned into a fatality.

One of the new, young chimps decided to challenge Jo-Jo, the older male. Jo-Jo had been living by himself for a long time, and without the benefit of growing up with his mother and family, he had no experience as to how to deal with this upsetting display of aggression. Jo-Jo also knew nothing about water, so when the young male came charging toward him, Jo-Jo was terrified and climbed over the railing meant to prevent the chimps from entering the trough of deep water.

The crowd and zookeepers watched in horror as the 130-pound chimp thrashed in the water. Jo-Jo disappeared three times under the water, each time surfacing and gasping for air. Finally the chimp went down and did not come back up again.

One of the distraught onlookers was Rick Swope. He and his wife brought their three daughters to the zoo every year. They were all watching the chimpanzees in their new enclosure when Rick saw Jo-Jo "flying through the air." He watched the whole dreadful scene unfold until he could watch no longer. He leapt over the fence and plunged into the murky water, swimming and feeling the bottom for the chimp's body.

His fingers finally located the chimp, and he managed to get Jo-Jo's dead weight over his shoulder. Rick made his way back to the chimps' island, and when he got to the steep shoreline, he struggled to push Jo-Jo's body up the bank. The crowd was screaming at Rick to come back because a group of agitated males chimps baring their canines were heading his way to investigate.

Rick started to retreat but stopped when he saw Jo-Jo's limp body sliding back into the water. The crowd continued to yell. He looked up at his family, beckoning him to return to safety, and then he looked down at Jo-Jo disappearing into the moat. Rick stood still for just a beat before going back in to rescue Jo-Jo.

Again, he heaved the heavy body up the slippery mud slope. Jo-Jo's body was motionless, but as Rick pushed him up the slope, the chimp made weak efforts to grapple his way along the ground. Rick held Jo-Jo's body above the water until the chimp rested on level ground, then jumped back over the fence.

A bystander with a video camera recorded the entire event, and that evening, footage of the incredible rescue was shown around the continent. Rick Swope was a national hero.

The director of the Jane Goodall Institute USA contacted Rick and said, "That was a brave thing you did. You must have known how dangerous it was. What made you do it?"

Rick replied, "Well, I looked into his eyes. And it was like looking into the eyes of a man. And the message was, 'Won't *anybody* help me?'"

In an interview with *Desert News*, Rick said, "Everyone in the whole place was just standing around watching this monkey drown. When he went down the second time, I knew I had to do something."

The 33-year-old truck driver did not fear for his life. "He was looking at me. I think he knew that I was helping him."

Rick received Jo-Jo's plea for help loud and clear and risked his life to help a fellow being who was in serious trouble. We are after all, close cousins with the chimpanzee. Perhaps this kinship binds us to depths we are not even aware of until put to the test.

This thought-provoking scenario forces me to ask myself, "Would I do the same?" I sincerely hope so.

Back to Nature

In Alberta, the Wildlife Rehabilitation Society of Edmonton is the only urban wildlife shelter, and it has been providing compassionate care for injured and orphaned wildlife since 1989. The society has helped thousands of birds and mammals receive medical treatment so they could eventually be released back to their natural habitat.

It is surprising that an industrialized city with over one million inhabitants would require the full-time services of a wildlife center, but this shelter operates 365 days a year, treating everything from songbirds, waterfowl and raptors to flying squirrels, muskrats and moose.

In the spring of 2007, the shelter admitted a rarely seen patient: a boreal owl. This owl ranks as one of the top five most wanted bird species on the North American birders list. They are not so sought after because they are endangered or threatened but primarily because of where they occur—they are typically only found in the coniferous boreal forests of the northern hemisphere. Also, their small stature (about 10 inches long) is well camouflaged with gray-brown plumage, so they blend in with the landscape.

This particular boreal owl had been hit by a car just outside of Edmonton. A woman driving down the highway noticed a group of crows surrounding a smaller bird on the side of the road. As animal lovers are prone to do, she slowed down to see what was going on, and a pair of beautiful yellow eyes looked right at her. She immediately pulled over. The crows scattered as she approached, and she could see that the owl was injured but alive. She gently collected it and drove straight to the Wildlife Rehabilitation Society of Edmonton.

The shelter tends to a lot of birds every year; 85 percent of their admissions are birds, and 15 percent of those belong to the raptor family, which includes hawks, falcons, eagles and owls. So the staff was not surprised to see an owl being brought in, but they were amazed to discover that it was a boreal owl. Alberta is one of the best places in the world to encounter this seldom-seen species, but Edmonton is not situated in the boreal forest. This owl had traveled quite a distance.

Kristin Arnot, Director of Wildlife Services, examined the owl immediately. Kristin determined that the bird's left shoulder was swollen but, luckily, was not fractured. That the owl had escaped with such a minor injury was remarkable considering that the car would have been traveling over 60 miles per hour when it hit her. She was placed in a small enclosure that would limit her movement. What this owl needed was the equivalent of bed rest to recover from her ordeal.

Though it seems an unlikely occurrence, there is a good explanation for how a bird and a car can collide. Drivers toss sunflower seeds, for example, out the window thinking they are biodegradable and will not harm the environment. The food can attract small mammals and birds that view the shells as a tasty snack. Now there is wildlife on the road, foraging for food.

The scenario with the boreal owl could have unfolded like this: a mouse decides to investigate some littered food; an owl, perched high in a tree, watches with interest from across the road; the owl swoops down across the highway to get the mouse and is hit by a car. Thousands of animals are injured or die each year because of being struck by a vehicle, and many times, it is because they were feeding. Litter and wildlife can be a lethal combination.

The staff and volunteers cared for the owl every day but were careful to limit their interaction. The only human contact she received was when she was fed or examined or when her enclosure was cleaned. Kristin explained, "Wild animals find it extremely stressful to be in captivity. They see us as predators. Ideally, we like to see our patients feisty and wanting nothing to do with us. This makes their release back into the wild very easy." If the animal gets habituated to humans, survival on its own becomes next to impossible.

Once the owl was healed, she was moved to a large enclosure outside, where she could get acclimatized to the outdoors and practice flying. Much like athletes, wild animals need to get their

A golden eyed boreal owl

stamina and strength back after an injury. She needed to exercise her shoulder and wing after her extended cage rest before being freed.

After six weeks, the little boreal owl was fit and ready to be released back into the wild. The shelter worked with local biologists from Alberta Fish and Wildlife to determine the best habitat for her release. They had no idea of the exact location of her former territory, so they needed to find an area that would meet her needs for nesting and hunting.

The owl was released in Wagner Natural Area, protected parkland outside of Edmonton. The district was richly diverse in both flora and fauna; the black spruce and white spruce forests, meadows and ponds made it ideal owl country. Once her cage was opened, the owl flew straight for the trees and did not look back, just the way it should be. This little girl was back home.

Creature Feature

During winter, the boreal owl hunts more prey then it needs, stowing the extra in tree nooks for later use. When the owl is ready to eat the reserves, it sits on the frozen prey to thaw it out first before ingesting.

Every Second Counts

Sometimes in life there comes a time when you can't just wait to see how things are going to turn out. You need to make a decision and act on it, especially when lives are at stake. And that's exactly what five men in the small coastal village of Seal Cove, Newfoundland, did when a pod of white-beaked dolphins became trapped in ice.

Residents first noticed the five dolphins on February 15, 2009. It is believed that the dolphins may have chased a school of fish into the harbor and became trapped when a storm pushed ice from the open Atlantic into the cove. As the water began to freeze over with "slob ice," a thick layer of slush and large frozen chunks of ice, the hole in which the dolphins were swimming and breathing began to shrink.

Winston May, the Mayor of Seal Cove, was concerned about the dolphin's welfare, as the Canadian Press reported: "They're not going to survive much longer. They keep going round in circles and trying to keep this little pool of water open so that they can have their breathing area."

The mayor acted quickly and contacted the Fisheries Department to see if an icebreaker could be sent to help free the dolphins. He was told that no vessels were available. Meanwhile, local residents flocked into his office in tears over the trapped animals.

Stanley Banks, a resident of Seal Cove, told the Canadian Press, "You could hear the screams coming out of them. And they were trying to break the ice there just to survive. And there's us empty-handed." Sixteen-year-old Brandon Banks had gone to bed each night listening to the wails of the five dolphins. It was distressing for everyone in the community.

The panicked animals continued to cry and circle frantically as the ice froze around them and the hole became increasingly smaller. Just 100 feet from the shoreline, residents watched helplessly as the animal's situation deteriorated.

Four days later, the situation was dismal; by morning there were only four dolphins left, and by midday the number had shrunk to three. It is feared that the two missing dolphins died from the stress and exhaustion of the ordeal.

After four nights of listening to the dolphins crying out in distress, five residents, including young Brandon Banks, took matters into their own hands. They acted on their impulse to do something instead of watching the animals perish.

Using a 17-foot boat with stainless steel propeller blades, the men set out to try and break up the ice, hoping to clear a path for the dolphins to escape. Rocking the boat back and forth, they painstakingly broke up the ice, creating a small path 820 feet long through the entrapping ice. Three hours later, they reached the small pool where the three remaining animals circled.

Two dolphins followed the boat as it led the way through the channel to the open ocean but one remained in the cove, too weak from the ordeal to follow. This part of the rescue would require a hands-on approach and a dose of courage.

Brandon didn't think twice before slipping into a survival suit and jumping into the frigid waters. He was now face to face with the eight foot marine mammal. The dolphin came up to him to rest its head, and Brandon helped keep the animal afloat so it could breathe through its blowhole. He told the Canadian Press, "I kept him up with my legs to keep his head up from under the water."

Mayor May said, "The dolphin just kind of attached to him and wrapped his flippers around him, more or less like a friend or mate." Brandon kept the almost 400-pound dolphin afloat while he gently wrapped a rope around its body.

The boat towed the dolphin slowly through the carved out channel. Once they hit the open ocean, the exhausted mammal seemed to have renewed energy. They loosened the rope and he swam off, returning to look at the men in the boat. The rescue mission took five hours to complete, and the reward was seeing the three dolphins swimming freely.

Residents reported seeing the three dolphins that evening in the outer, ice-free bay, swimming,

jumping around and feeding. They seemed healthier and stronger once they hit the open water.
Three dolphins were also spotted the following day
and, though it can never be proven, residents
believe that they were the rescued animals.

The mayor and the five rescuers, all born and
raised in this tiny town of 400 residents, were
declared heroes. "We had to do something because
if not, nobody was going to do [anything]," Banks
told the Canadian Press. "[The dolphins] would've
all died there."

These rescuers' act of compassion was both
humane and heroic. They followed their hearts
and acted instinctively, offering the same compassion to these sentient beings as they would have
offered a man lost at sea.

Creature Feature

Dolphins use echolocation to find food and to
navigate. They send out a beam of clicking
sounds that strike an object and are bounced
back to the dolphins, where they are detected
in an organ called the melon. The melon
decodes the echo, allowing the dolphins to
detect the size, shape, distance, speed and
direction of the object.

CHAPTER THREE

For the Love of Animals

If all the beasts were gone, men would die from a great loneliness of spirit, for whatever happens to the beasts also happens to the man. All things are connected. Whatever befalls the Earth befalls the sons of the Earth.

–Chief Seattle of the Suquamish Tribe,
in a letter to President Franklin Pierce

THERE IS NO LIMIT TO how far some folks will go for the love of an animal. One dear horse, by the name of Sweet Nothing, was blessed by the attention of several caring and compassionate helpers.

It all began when Roger Brincker purchased Sweet Nothing from a slaughterhouse to be a companion for one of his other horses. Roger operates Big Julie's Rescue Ranch, a sanctuary for cows, horses, mules and a variety of other creatures in southern Alberta. He spotted Sweet Nothing and thought she deserved a second chance.

Years later, Sweet Nothing suffered a leg injury, and after two surgeries, things were not improving.

The horse could no longer put any weight on her left hind leg, so she moved about on three legs.

Meanwhile, there was a couple with a deep interest in animal causes and welfare living about 100 miles from the ranch, in Calgary. Cindy Wasney and Dick Jackson heard about the ranch and collected food donations for the animals. In the summer of 2005, they delivered the food and met some of the residents. When the couple locked eyes with Sweet Nothing, she made an immediate impact on them.

"Cindy and I don't see a huge difference between the human animal and other animals," Dick explains. "When I met Sweet Nothing, I could imagine what it would be like to have a sore leg. I could see by looking into her eyes that she had spirit and she wanted to live. She was feisty. She wasn't ready to be put down."

Cindy spoke to the ranch's vet about their desire to help Sweet Nothing's medical situation. The vet recommended talking to Dr. Mattson at Moore & Company in Calgary, one of the largest equine veterinary services in Canada. Dr. Mattson consulted with a specialist at the San Luis Rey Equine Hospital in California, and together they decided her best option for a healthy and active future was to amputate the bottom part of her leg and build a prosthesis for her to wear.

Colman Prosthetics and Orthotics in Calgary normally make such devices for humans, but they

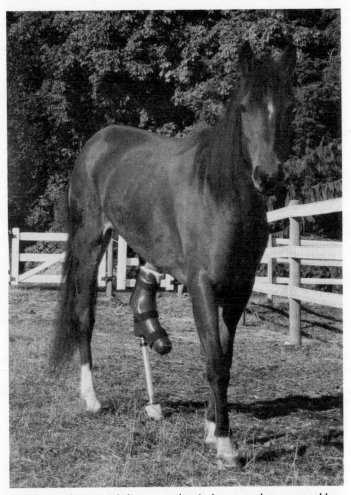

Sweet Nothing with her prosthetic leg wanders around her pasture.

were touched by Sweet Nothing's story and jumped in to help. The company designed, built and donated the prosthetic leg for the horse.

Dr. Mattson performed the surgery, and Sweet Nothing spent the next six months at Moore & Company, recovering and undergoing rehabilitation. The surgery and hospital care costs were covered by Cindy and Dick, and by funds raised though The Responsible Animal Care Society (TRACS) located in Westbank, British Columbia. A lot of people were rooting for the life of this horse.

During Sweet Nothing's recovery, Cindy and Dick moved to Victoria, British Columbia. When she was ready to be released, Roger and Dick transported her in a trailer to her new home, a farm offering green grass and year-round grazing.

Sweet Nothing had been given a new lease on life, not once but twice, because a group of people spread throughout the country believed she was worth it.

As Dick says, "We helped another fellow being."

Help Is On the Way

Help does not always come in the form of human assistance. Sometimes, a member of the animal kingdom leads the way.

Leslie L'Heureux and her family lived on a large acreage in Mayerthorpe, a small town in central Alberta. The family pets included a cat named Toby, two short-haired rabbits named Patches and Blackie, an old basset hound named Charlie and a five-year-old border collie cross, Riley. It was a full house.

Riley was a wonderful dog and as bright as they come. Leslie got him from the Second Chance Animal Rescue Society (SCARS), an organization dedicated to finding adoptive families for homeless and abandoned animals in Northern Alberta. She had seen his picture on their website and fell in love with him instantly. His sweet face, splotched with black and white markings, was irresistible.

Leslie remembers, "I thought he was the most beautiful dog I had ever seen. From the moment I saw his picture, I knew he was ours."

Border collies are known for their energy, lively spirit and intelligence. They are the ultimate herding dogs. These are working dogs, always on the job, making sure everything is fine with the herd or, in this case, the family pack.

Even though Riley had been abused, his nature was kind and his temperament loving. He bonded with Leslie right away and became her shadow. When she broke her leg and was bedridden for six weeks, it was her faithful friend Riley that lay in bed by her side, keeping her company the entire time. He seemed to know that she was in need of some tender, loving care, and he kept a careful eye on her.

Riley was protective of all his pack members, two-legged and four-legged. Leslie remembers peeking out her kitchen window, only to see her basset hound playing with a fox. The fox had obviously wandered into their yard from the nearby woods, and the fox and the dog happily chased one another around the fire pit.

Now, basset hounds are not generally known for their smarts; border collies, on the other hand, are. Riley knew in a heartbeat that Charlie should not be cavorting about with a fox. Who knew what the fox had in mind? Riley was not going to be bamboozled by this wily guy. He sprang to action and chased that fox right out of the yard.

Riley was a real character. He got on well with the other household pets, though he sometimes stuck his nose where it wasn't welcome. Toby, the cat, was a hunter at heart and spent an inordinate amount of time hanging out under the bird feeder, just in case there was an opportunity. Riley did not approve of her stalking ways and would intervene to let her know there would be no hunting on his watch.

The dog would place a heavy paw on the cat just as she was preparing to lunge for a bird, or if he needed to make his point more obvious, he'd open his jaws, placing his mouth over her head so she couldn't get to the birds.

The family's two domestic short-haired rabbits lived in a large hutch attached to a spacious pen. The pen walls were four feet high, so the rabbits could run and play in the grass and get plenty of exercise without escaping. During the day, the rabbits and Riley played together. They raced back and forth along the fence, taunting each other and stopping occasionally to nuzzle noses through the fence. At night, Leslie's 14-year-old son, Loden, locked the rabbits in their enclosed hutch.

One summer night in 2004, Leslie and her husband, Lennie, were awakened from a sound asleep. Riley always slept in their bedroom and was normally quiet and well behaved. On this particular night, though, something was wrong.

"Riley was carrying on, whining, barking," Leslie remembers. "He was agitated and moving around. Something was bothering him because he normally doesn't do that."

As she got up to let him out, she heard one of the rabbits scream. "I had never heard a rabbit let out a sound like that before. It completely shocked me. I opened the door and Riley shot out at a million miles an hour."

Her son had forgotten to lock the bunnies away, and a coyote had jumped over the fence into the rabbit pen. The coyote took off with Blackie between his jaws. Riley was running flat out behind him.

There was nothing Leslie and her husband could do. It was pitch black, and the animals had disappeared into the woods. The rabbit was gone, and Riley was nowhere to be seen.

Ten minutes later, Riley came trotting into the backyard. He was panting from the chase but was otherwise fine. There was no sign of the rabbit, and they feared the worst. The coyote must have killed Blackie. Leslie and her husband felt terrible. They knew how upset their son would be when they told him what had happened.

The following day, Lennie took off for work early. He checked the property; there was still no sign of the rabbit. A few hours later, Leslie opened the front door and couldn't believe her eyes. Sitting on their porch was Blackie, unharmed.

Riley must have chased down the coyote and harassed him. The threatened coyote probably decided the rabbit wasn't worth the trouble and released him. The rabbit was, after all, part of Riley's family, part of his pack. As Leslie said, they were friends.

It is still a mystery how the rabbit actually made its way back home. The family only had the bunnies for a month and never allowed them to run loose, so it's not as though the rabbits knew their way around the neighborhood. Perhaps the bunny followed Riley home and hid under the porch till morning. One thing is certain— Riley's brave move to get his fluffy buddy back saved the rabbit's life.

Leslie picked up Blackie and returned him to the hutch. Order had been restored, and life resumed as before. Riley, the SCARS rescue dog, a pooch that someone had mistreated and placed no value on, was a hero.

"Some people say you have to get a puppy to have a great, happy dog, but we are the opposite," Leslie says. "We think the greatest dogs are second-hand and would not have it any other way. He sure did know his home and who belonged in it. Riley was an amazing dog, the most incredible dog we have ever had."

Sleeping with the Caribou

Sometimes, the way we show our love for animals is through the work we do and the effort we invest. Field biologists and wildlife filmmakers experience many challenges working in the great outdoors: the frustration of not always getting the results they hoped for; the sacrifice of personal comfort and conveniences in rugged and remote locations; and the risk they face working in close proximity with wild animals, often in extreme weather conditions.

But, for these devoted souls, the collection of data, film footage and sound is all part of a bigger picture. Their investment of time and energy goes into documentaries and research papers that educate and inspire people to love and appreciate animals. That's what makes it all worthwhile.

Kathy Turco is a naturalist and is passionate about wildlife. She is both a biologist and a natural-sounds recording artist. Since 1986, Kathy has traveled the wilds of the north, capturing the sounds of wildlife.

She lives and works from her 20-foot-by-24-foot cabin, not far from Fairbanks, Alaska. Traveling all over the world, Kathy has recorded more than 2000 bird, mammal and habitat sounds—parrots in Mexico, guanacos in Chile and Adelie penguins in Antarctica—but her heart truly belongs to the creatures of Alaska.

Her impressive audio library boasts more than 800 hours of digitally recorded natural sounds, the majority of which represent life in the north: killer whales, muskoxen, bearded seals, bears, oyster-catchers and wolves.

"My mission," Kathy says, "is to give a voice to nature." She wants science to be interesting and stimulating and has made a profession out of eaves-dropping throughout the wilderness of Alaska.

Her sounds are heard in wildlife documentaries, Hollywood and IMAX feature films, and educational presentations in museums and aquariums around the world—presentations that celebrate the majesty of northern animal life. She hopes these projects inspire people to care about what they hear.

Recording natural sound is a feat few would ever consider tackling. It is arduous work, hauling a 50-pound pack with recording gear, a tent and other essentials across the tundra. Alaska is challenging: summer is short so everything is accelerated. There is a narrow window when the animals breed and give birth, for example, and if you miss it, you are out of luck for another year.

Then there's the matter of locating the creatures. It's not like they leave a copy of their travel plans so eager sound recorders can follow. Animals migrate and often settle in one area for only a short while before they are on the move again.

Travel is difficult up north—the area is vast with hundreds of miles between towns. Farther north is even less populated and remote, and there are no roads. To further complicate things, weather conditions are unpredictable. A weather front can move in without warning, forcing expedition plans to be postponed...again.

People who do this kind of work are driven by passion and obsession. Once Kathy sets her sights on an animal that she wants to record and add to her library, she goes after it with commitment and gusto.

Kathy had been trying for five years to capture the natural sounds of caribou, an iconic symbol of the north. And for five years, the caribou had eluded her. "Trips were weathered out, or their migration patterns changed just as I was about to hop on a plane. The trick is where to go and how to get there. You need luck to be in the right place and the right time."

Caribou are one of the most difficult animals to record because they are extremely restless and seem to always be on the move. Those precious moments when they actually bed down are few and far between, and only last for a short time. These animals have places to go.

The Alaska caribou population is almost one million strong. They travel in large herds, an impressive sight because they are the only deer where both the male and female have antlers. To witness the migration is incredible, thousands upon thousands of legs trekking across the tundra under a sea of antlers. In spring, caribou herds migrate hundreds of miles from winter ranges to their traditional calving grounds on the Arctic Refuge's coastal plain.

Kathy traveled in June 1994 to intercept and record the caribou, but once again her plans were foiled. She had found the caribou but couldn't get near them. Caribou are skittish, making them difficult to record. If you try to get near them, they bolt. If they sense anything is amiss—an alien sound or a movement—they are gone like the wind.

"You need to become invisible, become part of the landscape. The animals need to be comfortable before I can get the best recordings." She was feeling discouraged when she received a call from a bush pilot named Don.

"Don told me that he had an idea of how I might be able to get the recordings I was after. The caribou were moving from the north slope of Alaska's most northern mountains, the Brooks Range, located above the Arctic Circle, onto the coastal plain. Over the next several days, large groups of post-calving caribou who had gone into the mountains on their migration eastward into Canada would be headed back onto the plains to join the big herd."

"Don's plan was to locate the groups, then fly ahead, land on a gravel bar and throw me and my gear out of the plane onto the tundra, so I could set up my microphone and be zipped inside my tent before they passed by. That way the tent would look like part of the scenery."

His plan was good, though there were a few drawbacks. Kathy would be alone for several days in the middle of nowhere, zipped up in her tent like a sardine in a can. If anything went wrong, there would be no one to help.

The grizzlies were already on alert, anticipating the early caribou calves. Kathy always traveled unarmed—guns made her nervous. She carried bear spray and depended on her wits and instincts.

The plan went off without a hitch. She flew in a small plane for three hours from Fairbanks to the north side of the Brooks Range. Don picked her up in a smaller bush plane and flew her deeper into the wilderness. True to his word, he located the herd, landing just ahead of their path. He tossed his passenger and gear out of the plane, shouting "see you in the next weather front," before flying off.

Kathy put up her tent in record time and attached the microphone to a tripod outside the tent before climbing inside and zipping up. She had no sooner closed the zipper and put on her headphones when she heard the distant rumble of hooves. The caribou were coming.

The tent was a neutral gray, and to the caribou, apparently looked like part of the scenery, like a rock sitting on the plains. For three incredible days, groups of 500 to 1000 caribou paraded by her modest dome tent. She was smack in the path of the caribou's massive spring migration.

The Arctic sun was burning 24 hours a day, but Kathy lay blind in her cramped quarters. "I had no eyes, just super ears." Her tent was like an antenna and picked up every imaginable sound: the males' low grunts, the higher-pitched call of the females and the bleats of the calves; the distinctive "click, click" of their ankles joints as they walked by; the sounds of the animals eating and milling about.

Kathy did not leave the tent, nor did she crack the zipper for fear of spooking the animals. Absolutely everything—eating, sleeping and well, everything—happened in the tent. Kathy could not cook so her diet was meager—soybeans, bread and water. And when nature called, she relieved herself in a container. The mission was physically as well as mentally challenging. She could hear everything but wasn't always sure what she was listening to....

"You've got a microphone and your recorder, and you're lying there with your headphones on.

I'd fall asleep and wake back up again to sounds that would come and go. The wind plays with your mind; it's always moving. You swear you hear things. I was certain at one point that I heard voices. And I knew there were grizzlies out there waiting to feed on the calves. I'd hear a grunt and start imaging all sorts of things."

But dead quiet was equally unnerving. "When it was silent, there was not a single sound, just your heartbeat." It was the jolt of silence that offered Kathy the most moving moment she has ever experienced.

"I'd fall asleep when the caribou were migrating past the tent, and I must have dozed off. When I woke up, it was completely still and silent. I opened the zipper so very slowly, trying to not make a sound. I was lying on my belly and stuck my head out to see what was happening. I couldn't believe my eyes."

Kathy was surrounded by a herd of twenty caribou, and about seven of them had newborn calves. Most of the animals were sleeping, but the mothers and calves were talking to each other.

The mothers had dropped their calves on the calving grounds of the coastal plain but had headed into the mountains to escape the mosquitoes. Some years, the mountains provided relief from the deep, blowing snow of the coastal plain. Calving is an intense time for caribou, and the mothers normally give birth when the herd is gathered. The caribou know grizzlies are lurking nearby, hoping for an opportunity to feed on the new calves. There is safety in numbers.

"Seeing the mothers and these newborn calves was amazing. It was such a surprise because I didn't expect it. They were dozing and had no idea that I was there. There was such peacefulness. It was a gift and a privilege to be in their world. I put my head down on the tundra and wanted this moment to last forever."

Kathy nodded off back to sleep, and when she awoke the caribou were gone. Her five-year quest had been rewarded with the sounds of the migration and mothers nursing and tending their newborns. The wait was worth it. What an honor!

Kathy emerged from her nylon cocoon for the first time in three-and-a-half days. Dark clouds were rolling in from the Beaufort Sea. A storm was headed in her direction. Don would be coming for her; at least, she hoped he would be.

She quickly tore down her modest camp and sat on the tundra with the tent wrapped around her body and the poles in her hands. She was ready to either hop on the plane or get the tent back up fast. The storm was moving in quickly, and if Don didn't show, the tent was her only refuge.

"Here I was, standing in the middle of the tundra all alone with my tent wrapped around me. To my left, the sunlight was glistening off the mountain range and to my right, slow-moving 'ocean clouds' were moving in off the ice toward me. Snow was coming. I'm in the middle, just sitting there. For a flash, I felt like a child of the nomadic Inupiat people. Then I heard the buzz of the plane."

Kathy's caribou sounds have enhanced many film documentaries, radio programs and educational projects, all of which share the beauty of life in the Arctic National Wildlife Refuge. Her natural sounds are her tribute to a place she loves like no other. She wants to world to hear what Alaska and its inhabitants sound like.

"Nature gives me these gifts, and for me, every second is worth it."

Happy to See You Again

It takes courage, creativity and action to alter the course of destiny. For a gentle, loving rottweiler by the name of Roxy, Laura Dumas' and Trent Magis' determination and industrious spirits changed her life. Roxy was diagnosed with cataracts and at the tender age of four was destined for blindness.

With her cloudy, blue eyes, Roxy was starting to bump into furniture—and people. Laura's sister and brother-in-law had owned Roxy since she was five months old, but with two small children and another on the way, they were concerned about safety, both for Roxy and for their children. A bump by a beefy 69-pound dog can send anyone flying, and Roxy had recently cut her face walking into the fire pit. Sadly, things were going to get much worse as her condition advanced.

Laura and Trent were both finishing their secondary education, and though they did not have children, their house was full: they had Dante, their playful shepherd-lab-collie and two cats, Nea and Bandit. Roxy got on well with the other three critters and was such a good, loving girl that she was hard to resist. This was a rottie who enjoyed life to its fullest. After talking it over, they decided in May 2008 to adopt Roxy into their family.

Roxy could still see some shapes and distinguish objects that were high contrast. Her vision was decreasing quickly, though, and she frequently tripped on curbs, stumbled over uneven ground and bumped into poles, benches, people and other dogs.

"We tried with quite a bit of success," Laura says, "to train Roxy to step up curbs, over holes and down curb edges by using the words 'step' and 'hole.' She actually got quite good at this, and it was a feasible option when we took Roxy for a walk on-leash."

But at the off-leash dog park, she never heeded their warnings. Like a high-energy puppy, she ran around trying to keep up with Dante and the others, bumping into things or stumbling. Trent remembers, "It was obvious that we had to do something for Roxy's safety and quality of life."

They inquired about cataract surgery for dogs, learned that it was possible and that two places in Alberta performed the procedure. That was great news, but unfortunately, both clinics were in Calgary, and the couple lived more than three hours away in Edmonton. And the surgery would cost around $4000, well over budget for two students.

Laura remembers, "I was thinking about how girl guides and scouts collect bottles for their camping trips and jokingly said to Trent, 'we should collect bottles for Roxy.' What I didn't expect was that Trent would agree!"

The couple put their heads together and came up with a plan. They designed a website called "New Eyes For Roxy" that told Roxy's story, featured photos of the beautiful gal and asked anyone interested in helping to please donate their bottles. Alongside their bottle goal was an inspiring slogan: "Aiming for Two Eyes!"

By the beginning of July, they had posters asking for bottle donations hanging in all the dog parks. Laura remembers hanging the first poster at Roxy's favorite park. They pinned it up, then set off to stroll through the river valley. When they returned an hour later, 6 out of 10 phone number tabs had been taken. This was encouraging.

The couple asked friends, family and neighbors to help spread the word, too. The first batch of bottles was donated by the neighbors and fetched almost $500. Things were looking up for Roxy.

In total, more than 150 families donated bottles to "New Eyes For Roxy." Some offered spare change, and there were a few larger donations, as well. Names of the supporters were posted with a special thank you on the website.

Laura and Trent made many trips to the bottle depot, their small car stuffed with empties, plus three trips with a donated pickup truck and 18-foot trailer piled four feet high. Bottle collecting had taken on a whole new meaning.

"The response was extremely positive! We drove around Edmonton and areas, collecting whatever bottles people were willing to donate. After four months, and hundreds of hours sorting a garage full of overflowing bags and boxes in the middle of summer (yes, just imagine the smell!), we finally had collected, sorted, counted and hauled over 50,000 bottles, totaling nearly $5000."

They called the C.A.R.E. (Calgary Animal Referral and Emergency) Center in Calgary to make an appointment for the surgery. Roxy was booked for 7:00 AM on December 23, 2008, just two days before Christmas.

When her anxious owners picked her up at 4:00 PM the same day, she could see! What a gift for each of them. To add to the exhilaration, when they went to pay for Roxy's surgery, an additional sum of $250 had been anonymously donated to help with the bill.

The next day, Trent took Roxy for a walk and noticed that she tracked a magpie with her eyes, a huge difference from not being able to see a park bench or a fire pit. "Roxy continues to play like a puppy and finds enjoyment in everything she does. She has not bumped into anything since her surgery." Of course, now her roommate Dante can't sneak up and pounce on her anymore, and her feline siblings have a much harder time stealing her food.

Trent says, "This has been a great validation that there are lots of good people out there willing to help complete strangers, all to give a dog a new lease on life. Everyone who donated

Laura and Trent smile as Roxy now sees the world through new eyes.

was a dog lover, so it's easy to understand their generosity—we've all been touched by the companionship, loyalty and unconditional love shown us by our best friends."

They held a "thank you" party at Roxy's favorite park three months after her surgery and handed out dog biscuits to all her canine pals. Laura and Trent were so touched by the acts of kindness their plea received that they wanted to give something back. With the excess money raised, they are hoping to establish a charitable fund to help other dogs in need.

Yes, it will be a bottle drive, because this one certainly delivered a miraculous outcome: the gift of sight.

~∞~

Section Two

The Joy of Animals

*Animals share with us the privilege
of having a soul.*

—Pythagoras

Animals make life so interesting. It seems that we are fascinated by how different they are from us, yet perplexed and awestruck at how much we are alike. We are all members of the animal kingdom, so we share many likenesses—give or take a tail or a wing. Our curiosity pushes some of us to go to great lengths to observe animals, to get close to them and try to get to know them. The presence of animals makes our lives better in so many ways.

Like most kids, I was curious about wild animals, the ones that weren't allowed in the house. I absolutely adored those fuzzy black-and-yellow-striped caterpillars (yes, the ones that munch on your poplar and maple trees). This is the caterpillar of the spotted tussock moth, also called the yellow woolly bear. How could I not fall in love with a critter with a name like that?

I used to gather up a handful of the creatures and put them in a sewing basket with some leaves. I named them all George and would sit and watch them for an hour or two before putting them back outside. This was all fine and dandy until one day I left the lid of the sewing box open and all the Georges escaped, just as my parents' dinner party guests were arriving. Yes sir, bringing the wildlife into the house was fascinating....

Animals have a great capacity to make us laugh and brighten our day. We are amused by their curious nature, the predicaments they get themselves into and, sometimes, the quandaries we find ourselves facing because of them. And sometimes they show another side, one of compassion, empathy and kindness.

I bow to the members of the animal kingdom for their grace, their goodness and the smiles they bring to our human lives.

CHAPTER FOUR

Close to Home

The love of all living creatures is the most noble attribute of man.

—Charles Darwin

AT ONE TIME OR ANOTHER, most of us have enjoyed the company of a pet. A dog, cat, bird, maybe even a hamster or snake. These are pretty common relationships, and nobody is going to raise their eyebrows if they drop by your house for a visit.

Sometimes, though, when you least expect it, things on the home front can get a little wilder. My grandmother lived at the edge of the city limits near a treed area. She was always finding homeless and injured animals; everybody was welcome at her house. One spring day in the '70s she rang my mom and said, "You'll never guess what I've got downstairs."

Two furry muskrats had crawled into her basement through the window she had left ajar for the cats. It was a perfect setup for what would become

"The Muskrat Spa and Motel." There was even a stepladder at the base of the window for easy access.

My grandmother contacted the Alberta Society for the Prevention of Cruelty to Animals (SPCA), but they told her it would take a few days before they could come by to pick up the animals. So, she made the pair comfy. She filled a metal washtub with water so they could bathe and take a dip, laid out a spread of fruits and veggies, made them a bed of blankets and spread out some paper. The muskrats had a grand time frolicking about in her basement. They'd never had it so good.

Four days later the wildlife officer arrived, put the muskrats in a crate and released them back into the woods. The next spring, the critters were back. Seems as though my grandmother's hospitality was so good that they decided to visit her resort again.

But sometimes these wild creatures come into our lives and stay; they remain long enough to become part of the family. Human lives become part of their world just as the animals' lives blend into ours. When the call of the wild is close to home, it is a guarantee that lives will be touched and changed forever.

Had Cat, Did Travel

Few people rouse one's memory bank better and fetch a more enthusiastic response than Al Oeming. For millions of Canadians, this man literally brought the "wilds of Africa" to rural communities. Traveling throughout Canada from coast to coast and into the northern territories and Alaska, Al and his cheetah, Tawana, made quite a stir.

He is likely the only person on Earth that has, or ever will, journey beyond the Arctic Circle with a cheetah. For those who had the privilege of meeting Tawana in Inuvik, Northwest Territories— Land of the Midnight Sun—it is a vivid memory like no other. I don't think it's possible for an African cheetah to be farther away from its native home, nor could one have been more loved than Tawana was on that occasion.

Al's interest in touring with Tawana was simple: he wanted to show people the natural world while encouraging environmental awareness and conservation. A fervent lover of nature and all living things, Al held a masters of science degree in zoology. He decided to share his passion for animals by opening a private zoological park.

On August 1, 1959, Al opened the gate to the Alberta Game Farm. Located just 15 miles east of Edmonton, Alberta, the game farm was home to an incredible 3200 animals representing 86 species. He had gathered the most impressive collection of hoofed animals (ungulates) in the world, with herds of bison, caribou, muskox, Dall sheep, zebra and the only breeding herd of Rocky Mountain goats in captivity. The game farm also contained an assortment of carnivores including cougars, wolves, lynx, snow leopards and Siberian tigers; flocks of pheasant, crane and geese; exotics such as hippos, rhinos and mountain gorillas; and northern mammals such as wolverines, grizzly bears and polar bears.

The Alberta Game Farm was the largest private zoological park in Canada and the second largest in North America. There were no pavilions or large buildings typical of today's zoos and parks, just 1500 acres of rolling aspen parkland and the wide-open expanse of the great outdoors. The exhibits were large, fenced enclosures, and the herds of ungulates had spacious areas to roam.

Al was interested in creating breeding programs for endangered species and had rare animals such as the Pallas' cat from Russia and the yellow-throated marten from Asia on exhibit. He was also curious about how tropical animals would fare in a colder climate and found they adapted well.

The Alberta Game Farm was an important part of my childhood. I will always remember the day an animal keeper let me bottle-feed a grizzly cub through the fence. I was an animal-crazy kid, and Al Oeming and his family of animals was the next best thing to being in the wild. His amazing facility influenced my decision to pursue a zoology degree and work with animals.

In 1981, Al phased out the warm-weather exotics, and the Alberta Game Farm became known as Polar Park. The park featured animals indigenous to cold climates and continued to captivate the public until it closed its doors in 1998.

For 39 years, thousands of people from around the world were able to visit Al Oeming's wildlife haven and view animals they may never have had a chance to see anywhere else. While visitors were traveling to see the wildlife in his park, Al decided to take things one step further by taking a wildlife experience to the people. Every fall, Al and his prized cheetah, Tawana, hit the road and toured until spring.

He wanted to give the public something they had never seen before—something that would touch the hearts and souls of the people and create an interest in nature without being "too sermonizing." Visiting communities and more schools than he could keep track of, Al and his majestic seven-foot-long, 110-pound cat left a lasting impression on anyone they encountered.

Tawana's good nature was typical of cheetahs. Al told me, "Cheetahs are the tamest animals on Earth. Tawana would yawn in the middle of an earthquake!" Tawana was relaxed wherever he went: he enjoyed curling up on the living room sofa for a catnap at home just as much as flopping down on a hotel bed to stretch out and relax in one of the countless rooms he shared with Al on the road.

Al Oeming and his beloved cheetah, Tawana

Al wanted to offer children and adults an experience that would stick with them—and he succeeded. Just say the name "Al Oeming" in Canada, and there is a good chance you will be met with wide eyes, a bright smile and a spilling of words about the time "the cheetah came to my school."

Dan Fortin will never forget the day Al and Tawana showed up at his school in Zenon Park, Saskatchewan. It was a cold, prairie winter day but that didn't stop people from traveling to the community hall.

"It was the '60s," Dan remembers, "and here we are in this tiny hamlet in northern Saskatchewan. Country folk had only heard about Africa and seen pictures in books of lions and cheetahs. Al made it all real. No one could believe it; he might as well have brought a dinosaur. He changed the lives of these people. It was something they would never have had a chance to see in their lives. I'm 51 years old and I will always remember that day. It was one of the greatest things that ever happened to our little community."

By visiting communities and through his animal parks and a variety of film and television projects, including *Al Oeming: Man of the North*, Al brought wildlife practically to the doorstep of many people.

Here is a story written by Al Oeming about life on the road with Tawana, his gorgeous, big-eyed cheetah:

Crisscrossing Canada as an itinerant naturalist for 40 years, I've acquired a mountain of memories. My mission on these annual tours was primarily to bring into the lives of young people a message, a plea, to fully appreciate the natural world. Even in my early years of lecturing, I quickly discerned that schools were a fertile ground for every type of crusader. There was a variety of speakers including policemen, firemen, first aid professionals, career counselors, safety inspectors, those espousing religion—the list went on and on. Few were inspiring speakers and most failed to arouse the students. Many teachers lamented the fact that the majority of the school kids were simply not interested. Something was missing.

I spent some careful time pondering this issue. My goal was to present a program that would open the hearts and minds of young and old alike. It would take more than a human presence. My decision was made, and henceforth my traveling partner in all my engagements would be Tawana, a beautiful, tame cheetah. Why a cheetah? Cheetahs are a threatened species, they are the embodiment of grace and, when raised from early kittenhood, they become one of the tamest animals known to humans. Every youngster already knew that the cheetah was the "King of Speed," an incredible runner and, in fact, the fastest land mammal on Earth. The cheetah has a romantic history. Since time immemorial, it has been revered for its beauty and friendly manner. Cleopatra had tame cheetahs in her palaces, as did many of the princes of India. Tawana would be my magic door opener and charmer.

My program makeup was patterned like this: A tour was arranged for a specific region of Canada—the Peace River region of Alberta is an example. An evening lecture with a 90-minute, top quality nature film and Tawana in attendance became standard practice. I provided live narration for every showing because I was telling a story and delivering a message that I passionately believed in. My hope was that I could touch the public pulse with my oratory. In a large territory like the Peace Country, 30 or more towns were booked for public evening performances. A nominal admission fee was charged. School gyms were the most suitable for my purposes. I wanted the largest hall in town and was determined to fill it to capacity. School principals were warmly receptive to the program and offered full cooperation. Most of the larger towns had an average of six or more smaller schools in the district. The principal of the school where the public lecture would be held and I worked out a daily school visitation schedule whereby I would appear with Tawana and speak to the students. Prior to this, posters were put up throughout the town, and all available advertising venues were covered. The students were primed for the visit and excitement was at fever pitch. The schedule was tight, and we had to move with the speed of a cheetah to make sure no school was missed. All school performances were free.

Students were assembled in the hall. A microphone and a carpeted table for Tawana were set up. Curtains were drawn, and Tawana and I were behind the curtain as the principal made the introduction. The curtains parted, and Tawana purred as loud as an idling motorcycle into the mike. What a moment it was with the students' eyes bulging like protruding doorknobs.

Some of the most unforgettable moments in my life came from simply witnessing the sheer joy and fascination in those young faces. The time with the students included a question and answer session pertinent to the wildlife in their region. A short life story of Tawana and some real-life anecdotes of hilarious adventures on the road ensued. My talk concluded with the statement that a cheetah, when tamed, becomes so fond of people that he meets any stranger as a good friend. To illustrate this point, I gazed across the assembly and said I was looking for that perfect stranger to come up and pet Tawana. Making that choice was difficult with not one hesitant kid in the crowd. The lucky kid would come up and gently scratch Tawana behind the ears, and in response Tawana would turn on his majestic purr. The students were told that if they came to the evening show that night, we would let everyone pet the cheetah so they should be sure to bring to their cameras. A sold out evening audience was guaranteed whether it was −40° winter weather or not. It was truly a glorious moment in a rural farm family's life when they got a photo taken with their children sitting next to Tawana. I frequently meet people in every part of Canada who remember in vivid detail meeting Tawana. One lady made me feel it was all worthwhile when she told me that experience enriched her life forever.

Tawana enjoying some hands-on attention

Aside from classroom appearances and evening lectures, other quite unexpected events added to the color of the tours. Let me preface this one story with a further insight into Tawana's daily routine on the road.

Tawana dined on a carefully controlled diet of top quality beef. Often my assistants bemoaned the fact that Tawana dined on T-bone steak while we settled for baloney. He was, after all, the real star of this show, and he was treated like royalty. Exercise was essential each day without fail, be it rain or shine or howling blizzard and −45°. In southern Saskatchewan, it was a cheetah-made setup—wide-open prairie with no fences and an abundance of fleet-footed jackrabbits. In other regions, to exercise Tawana, we had to find a relatively quiet stretch of road. We substituted an ordinary sweep broom for a jackrabbit. The broom was tied to a 40-foot length of rope and attached to the rear bumper. Tawana would be positioned well ahead of our car broom, preferably over a small hill to ensure the vehicle was out of his sight. I would wait with Tawana at the side of the road and let him tear loose as soon as the car passed. A fast mile with Tawana running at full speed maintained his incredible physical condition. Hence, any time he saw a broom he exploded.

The location was southern Saskatchewan. The school was located on the edge of town on a treeless plain. My crew was behind the curtain awaiting the entry of the students when Tawana's keen eyesight spotted the school janitor with his broom in action, pushing out the last of his sweepings through the open back door. Students were now pouring in from the front end. They saw a spotted streak racing toward the janitor. The janitor looked up to see Tawana racing toward him. With broom in hand, he raced out the back door with Tawana in hot pursuit. I could not get out of the building because the students were piled up watching the action outside. One little chap watching it unfold moved back and said to me, "Mister, there's a big cat chasing Jake, and that cat is doing 70 miles an hour but Jake is doing 80!"

Jake was indeed setting a new world record for the short sprint. All Tawana wanted was the broom, and he had it. Jake was still running and quickly fading into the winter skyline. A conservationist's life on the road was never dull.

My tour dispensed biological knowledge, enjoyment and a reverence for nature with a generous dash of humor periodically thrown in.

Creature Feature

The cheetah is the fastest mammalian sprinter on Earth and can reach 45 miles per hour within 2.5 seconds. Its top speed is up to 64 miles per hour. For more than half of every stride, the cheetah is airborne. The "tear marks" at the inner corners of its eyes tell you that you are looking into the eyes of a cheetah, not a leopard.

Daycare Gone Wild

Some people in this world enjoy the company of animals as much as they do the company of people. They seem to intuitively understand what animals need and even what they are trying to communicate. Delia Gruninger is exactly that kind of animal-loving soul. Delia and animals are simpatico. They quite naturally belong together.

From the time she was a young girl, Delia dreamed of becoming a zookeeper. She pursued her goal and has been caring for and training animals at the Edmonton Valley Zoo in Edmonton, Alberta, since 1981. Her passion for animals reached further, though, and over the years, her home has welcomed two-legged, four-legged and winged infants.

Sometimes, Mother Nature doesn't get it quite right. Mothers occasionally abandon newborn babies or are unable to care for them, and a trained animal caretaker is needed to provide attention and supervision around the clock.

Delia hadn't been at the zoo long when a female Capuchin monkey gave birth but was unable to feed her new baby because she lacked milk. Delia offered to take responsibility for the baby. Caring for the wee being was a big job. He needed to be fed every two hours, required constant supervision and, of course, had to go home with her every day at the end of her shift. Delia was committed to the task.

She didn't mention this little tidbit to her husband, Larry, so when he got home that night, he had a surprise waiting. Beaming with excitement she told him, "I have a baby."

Larry was also an animal lover and was completely on board with her decision. Just like that, Larry became a surrogate dad and helped in the day-to-day care of the baby monkey, named Buttons.

While Delia sewed batches of diapers to accommodate a tail, Larry helped prepare bottles, and he babysat on those rare occasions when Delia was without her monkey. During the cold winter months, Delia wore a red one-piece hunting suit so she could zip the baby snugly inside. It wasn't a great look but, hey, it got the job done.

Everywhere Delia went, Buttons went—usually strapped to her in a snugly baby carrier. In Delia's words, "It was our life, and Larry loved it. To experience the love you get from an animal is so unconditional...they are so beautiful."

Buttons slept beside his foster parents' bed in a basket. That is, until one day the little rascal was able to hop out of his bed and right into theirs. After the Gruningers raised Buttons for one year, the monkey was ready to join his family again. Delia, with the help of her husband, had done her job well and now it was time for Buttons to start hanging out with other monkeys.

One year later, the Gruninger home was welcoming a baby ape: a white-handed gibbon named Lily. Once again, life revolved around a little bundle of fur—this time one with a human-like visage and needs even more similar to a human baby's needs than to those of Buttons the monkey. As before, Larry assisted Delia with all the tasks of cleaning, feeding and babysitting. This lucky ape had two doting surrogate parents.

The couple still howls with laughter about the night they bundled up baby Lily, now almost two months old, to attend Christmas Mass. With Lily wrapped in blankets like all the other babies in church, they quietly slipped into a pew at the back.

Delia was struck with panic as she watched all the other mothers unwrap their babies in the warm church. Polite attendees were asking to see the "little baby." After initial protests, Delia finally revealed the hairy, little ape face. It was quite a shock for those baby-seekers!

A few years later, Delia had a baby of her own, a son the couple named Dustin. A little girl named Brittney came along a couple years after that. Delia was truly "Super Mom"—a full-time zookeeper and a full-time mother, with critters of every description coming and going as needed: primates, a variety of other mammals and birds.

She even took on a wallaby, a bouncing marsupial native to Australia. Baby wallabies are raised in their mother's pouch so—I'll bet you can see where this is going—Delia designed a cloth pouch for her first hopping ward. Karma the wallaby spent eight months secured to Delia's tummy.

Delia's skills as a surrogate marsupial mother paid off; Karma grew into a healthy, sociable wallaby and was returned to her family. This was a good trial run for Delia because there would be others hopping in Karma's footsteps through the front door of the Gruninger home.

As soon as Delia's children were old enough, they joined in with the feeding and helped to watch over their roommates with the caring eyes of siblings. One year, the family had two baby otters over the summer. The kids loved to fill the baby pool and watch the otters swim and play in the water.

Then there was Beau, the beaver. She was brought to the zoo as an orphan so tiny that she could fit in the palm of your hand. Fully furred and equipped with a teeny, scaly tail, Beau paddled about the bathtub as the kids watched over her. What an education for these children and for the critters that had two more caring souls looking out for them.

There were also birds that needed fostering. Delia incubated eggs, raised shorebirds and even cared for a little saw-whet owl. It's not everyday that you walk into a living room and see an owl happily perched in a hibiscus tree.

Delia is proud of her family's support. "I could never have done this without the help of my entire family. It's a big job, and they helped make it all possible. My life has always been about the zoo. Every page of our photo album is interspersed with animals."

Karma the Wallaby hanging out with Peatree

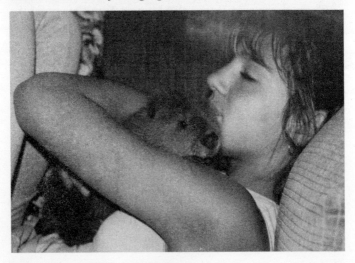

Baby Beau cuddling with Brittney

Caring for animals is a lot of hard work and requires a ton of energy. There are many sleepless nights with feedings and countless times when a night out or a weekend getaway is replaced with bottle-feedings, babysitting and the never-ending task of cleaning.

Delia smiles as she remembers, "I would disinfect the bathtub so the kids could take a bath. Then I'd disinfect it again so the otters or the beaver could go for a swim. There was always something to clean!"

"My kids and husband really loved helping to care for these animals. It makes me feel good knowing that these animals have gone on to educate and share their beauty with thousands of school children and visitors at the zoo."

Delia has been Mother Goose and Doctor Doolittle to dozens of animals. "It has been a privilege for me to be a part of these animals' lives," she shares. "It has given me experiences and allowed me to grow in ways that I couldn't have done any other way."

After 28 years of sharing their lives with all sorts of critters, her husband, Larry, still asks, "When are you bringing home another baby?"

Birds of a Feather

It seems as though the world is divided into two types of people: those that find stuff and those that lose it. Every time my mom takes her pooch for a walk, she finds something lying on the sidewalk or in the grass at the park. You name it—sunglasses, jewelry...all sorts of things. She keeps it all in a basket thinking that one day she'll stumble upon the owner.

My grandmother, Elsie, was exactly the same, only she found living, breathing animals; injured dogs on the side of the road, a cat with its head stuck inside an oil can—the list goes on. She brought them home with her, of course, to be tended to and nursed back to health.

And once they were in the house, they never left. Why would they? It was heaven. There were bowls of fresh cream, tuna and steak for snacks, plus a weekly car trip to the neighborhood fast-food drive-in to gobble down an ice-cream cone. Hey, if I were a cat or a dog, I'd want to live at my grand-mother's, too.

It seems that her great niece, Carol Kohlhofer of Campbell River, British Columbia, has the same uncanny knack for attracting animals, but in her case it's birds, and she insists "they find her." Together with her husband, Bruce, Carol has been rehabilitating wild birds since 1992.

The goal was always the same—to heal the birds so they could be released back into the wild. And when the Kohlhofers weren't sure if a bird was ready to be released, their little white zebra finch, Kasper, let them know.

Kasper was like a "little angel" whenever they had a bird in the house to rehab. Carol says, "She would perch on the edge of the box and watch the other bird. When a rehab was well enough, she always seemed to know. She would hover over the other bird and prompt it to fly off with her. Off they'd fly across the room, up to the valance in the living room. That was always our cue that the rehab could be released."

Carol has a soft spot for crows. They are intelligent birds, but it is more than that. She admires their parenting skills and their devotion to their young. Crows form a strong bond with their little ones, teaching them how to fly, bringing food to the nest and protecting them with fierce commitment. Carol has been dive-bombed many times by crows screaming for reinforcements when she has ventured unwittingly near a baby that has fallen from its nest to the ground. In Carol's eyes, crows are honorable birds.

Carol and Bruce's property is lush with trees and bushes, so birdwatching goes with the territory. Birds come and go all day long, much to the Kohlhofers' delight. But in June 1996, they noticed a baby crow in their backyard that did not seem quite right: it had a pink abscess protruding from the inside of its ear.

A few days later, Carol saw that the baby's neck was twisting to the side and its head was swinging slowly. The parents continued to try to feed it, but it was becoming more difficult to put the food into its beak because of the angle of its head. Something was wrong, but every time Carol tried to get close, the little crow flew onto the neighbor's roof.

One morning when Carol and Bruce left the house, the baby was nowhere in sight. They thought that it had probably died. But when they returned home at dusk, a few crows cawed and dove at them. Carol knew there must be a baby crow somewhere on the ground, and she was right.

She found the bird and raced into the house with it, ducking to avoid the distraught crows swooping down at her. Her intent was to see if there was anything she could do to help the baby bird. What she didn't realize was that this would be the start of a five-month rehabilitation journey, and the reward would be a long, healthy relationship with a wild black crow, one that would enrich their lives in ways they could never have imagined.

Carol examined the fledgling. It was the bird she had noticed with the abscess in its ear. There was no doubt that the bird was gravely ill. One eye was swollen shut, and a patch of feathers was worn away from the top of its head. When she found the bird, its head was on the ground and it was spinning its body around in circles. Carol held the bird up, and its head swung in a semi-circle back and forth.

Carol and Bruce decided to pierce the abscess, so Bruce sterilized a needle. Once the swelling had emptied, the head swinging stopped. It was a good start, but this crow had a long way to go before it was stable. The bird could not stand, so they used a laundry basket to make a cozy bed where it could be propped up to rest.

The bird's nostrils, called ceres, were full of infection. Carol cleaned the area throughout the day so it could drain and watched over the bird like a mother hen, doing everything she could to help it along. She named the crow Edgar Alan Poe, but learned later on that *he* was actually a *she*.

Carol and Bruce were devoted to nursing Edgar back to health, but there were several rough nights for both the bird and her caretakers. Many times Carol was sure the bird would not make it. "I dreaded opening the door to the laundry room where we kept her basket. I was sure she had died in the night. But, there she stood. 'Caw' she shouted at me. I knew she had a strong will to live."

After a month, Carol decided it would be good for the bird to have some fresh air and sunshine, so she carried the laundry basket with Edgar into the backyard. Edgar's mother was perched on the roof above the yard and looked down with interest. Carol gently placed Edgar on the grass. The bird was still unable to walk; she lost her balance and toppled over. The mother let out a blood-curdling scream that Carol will never forget. Carol quickly scooped up the bird and gave her some food and water. The upset mother seemed appeased and became silent. The mother crow continued to fly by every day and "check up" on the situation, but she never shrieked at Carol again.

The couple could not find an avian veterinarian in their area, and they had contacted the conservation officer but had not heard back, so they depended on home remedies and common sense to nurse the bird. Sometimes they were truly "winging it," but after five months, Edgar's infections finally cleared up; her neck was straightening, and she could finally walk around without toppling over. The swollen eye had opened, though there was still a bump over the eyebrow. One thing that did not change was Edgar's healthy appetite; even during the height of her illness, she gobbled up her dinner and then begged for food from their supper plates.

Over the five months, Edgar never tried to fly; in fact, it seemed that she was afraid of heights. She spent all her time walking around on the floor during the day, and at night she was tucked into her basket. There was no possibility that this bird could ever be released into the wild. So Carol and Bruce did the next best thing: they took Edgar outside every day during summer and fall. The yard was fenced, and there was a container of water that she loved to bathe in.

The crow became attached to both Carol and Bruce. "Edgar enjoyed my massages on her forehead above her ceres," Carol remembers. "As soon as I held her head in my hands and massaged that area, she would let out a big sigh—'Aaaah'—and completely relax her head and neck."

Friends and relatives who had originally thought that Edgar would not survive now thought it was a miracle that she had lived and was "almost normal." Edgar Alan Poe had fought hard for her life and had a personality as big as her name.

"Edgar was very playful," Carol recounts. "I'd play hide-and-seek with her, although I changed the name to 'hide-and-peck.' I'd dash around the corner of the foyer and wait. She'd walk and flap her wings after me. When she saw me, she'd bop my foot with her beak. Then she'd run away as fast as she could."

Carol gives Edgar a sip of water.

Crows are known to be sociable birds, and Edgar showed great affection toward her human companions. As the years went by, the antics continued. One day Carol was off to a frenzied start. She had been called to work that afternoon and had an appointment in the morning, so she decided to make a casserole ahead of time for supper. As she was taking out a canister of flour, she slipped and landed on her bottom. The flour, of course, was everywhere. She thought, "I'll just put a pot of water on to boil, and then clean up the mess."

On the way to the stove, Carol tripped over Edgar, who had a habit of following her around the kitchen. Water sloshed out of the pot and onto the flour-coated floor, creating a gooey, white paste. Carol was horrified; Edgar was delighted. She took it as a bathing opportunity, flapping her wings through the muck with glee. What a mess! Carol promptly washed the floor and cupboards and then cleaned the bird. By now Carol had a headache, and she needed to leave for her morning appointment and then head off to work.

By the time she got home that evening, she had a pounding migraine. Edgar was a gregarious gal and liked to spend time with people. She had the run of the kitchen, and Bruce had installed a baby gate to keep her out of the carpeted living room. Edgar, like most crows, was a vocal bird and often cried and cawed when Carol left the room—not a good thing when your head is aching. But, Carol had a plan....

"I laid down flat on my back—my head was throbbing. I figured that Edgar would put her head on my chest, and I would just cuddle her. I heard her claws tick, tick, tick on the floor coming toward me. All of a sudden, I felt my diamond stud earring being plucked from my ear! Oh my God! There it shone in her beak. She pranced about, and I'm on all fours chasing her around the floor. It was a game to her. Then she whirled around, looked at me and swallowed my earring. This had to be the worst day ever."

Carol never did make the casserole. Instead she checked the bird's droppings throughout the evening in search of her diamond. The next morning she saw a glint in Edgar's basket. The crow had regurgitated the earring. Carol remembers, "My stud was all polished and looked brand new."

Edgar loved to cuddle up with Bruce, too, and he would pat her and scratch her neck. The big, black crow was always up for a game, and the two would play together. She loved newspaper and would fold, twist and tear it, or ride on it as it was being pulled around the kitchen. Edgar's favorite times of the week were Friday and Sunday mornings—the days that Bruce was in the kitchen preparing French toast, one of her favorite treats.

The crow had lived with Carol and Bruce now for six years and was enjoying a happy, healthy life. But in November 2002, Carol noticed that Edgar's bad eye was inflamed and weeping, and she was rubbing it. An avian rehabilitation center had opened in a nearby town, so Carol and Edgar paid it a visit.

The vet examined Edgar as Carol relayed the story of how they had saved her. The vet said the condition that Edgar had suffered from was quite common in baby crows, and it was a "miracle" that they had been able to save the bird. Without antibiotics and an operation, there is only a three percent survival rate because the infection usually travels straight to the brain.

The examination revealed that Edgar had glaucoma in the infected eye as a result of the trauma she had suffered so many years ago. Removing the eye was the best option. The examination and blood work showed that the crow was healthy—she stood 16.5 inches high and weighed one pound. Edgar had an excellent chance of surviving the surgery. Carol, of course, was worried sick, but a few hours after the operation, once anesthetic wore off, she and her pet crow went home.

Over the years, Carol and Bruce acquired other feathered rescue creatures: Kricket, a naked little blob with sealed eyes that turned out to be a newly hatched house sparrow, and Yackie, a young, malnourished crow that suffered from epileptic-like fits. Their wild avian family was growing, and the Kohlhofers' were becoming skilled at rehabilitating injured and sick birds.

In May 2005, Edgar, now nine years old, made another trip to the vet, this time to have a tumor removed from her foot. Edgar was back on the operating table, and Carol was once again sobbing. Edgar was the Kohlhofer's baby and was a much-loved member of the family. The vet removed the growth between the bird's toes and tendons, hoping that he had got it all, but only time would tell.

Carol remembers, "Everyone wondered why we just didn't 'put her under.' But how could we? She was part of our family. We had to try to save her."

Edgar recovered and carried on as before in the company of her feathered mates Kricket and Yackie. By now, Carol had discovered a company that made "avian diapers," an invention that she describes as "a real godsend."

On the morning of June 8, 2008, Edgar was not looking like herself. Carole sensed that the crow was dying and had little time left. Cradled in Bruce's arms, Edgar Alan Poe, the most extraordinary crow, passed away at the age of 12. Carol and Bruce could feel tumors all over her body, but that strong will to live had kept her going.

This friendly crow had lived a full life and had shared an exceptional bond with Carol and Bruce. Carol describes Edgar as "...a beautiful, loving, affectionate soul. We miss her terribly. She was like a child to us." Edgar was buried in the backyard under the rose bush where she used to like to sit and rest each summer.

Carol maintains that injured, abandoned and orphaned birds "come to us" so they can be healed and, when possible, set free. The release doesn't always go according to plan. In the spring of 2009, Yackie the crow turned seven and Kricket the house sparrow turned 10. It seems that these two wild ones had no intention of leaving. In fact, Yackie used to circle the house, banging on the windows for Carol to let him back in every time she tried to set him free. There will be no "empty nest syndrome" in this household—even if Yackie and Kricket could be convinced to embrace freedom, the couple also owns four parrotlets and two lovebirds, along with a rescued canary and cockatiel.

Creature Feature

Crows are considered among the most intelligent birds in the world. They have an evolved language and can imitate sounds made by other animals, including the human voice. These corvids are social and live in family groups.

CHAPTER FIVE

Lend a Helping Paw, Hoof or Flipper

Only if we understand can we care. Only if we care will we help. Only if we help shall they be saved.

–Jane Goodall

FOR SOME OF US, ANIMALS are so much more than just creatures to admire and appreciate from afar. They play a significant role in our lives and are tightly woven into the essence of our day and perhaps even our jobs.

Animal-assisted therapy uses domesticated animals to help treat people with a variety of conditions—physical, emotional and mental. These animals seem to really care and want to share their kind dispositions and affection with those who need it. They appear to have insight, an awareness of the circumstances that afflict some people.

On occasion, this good, gentle spirit is found in the wild, and an untamed animal extends itself to help another living soul—animal or human—of its own volition. The animal seems to show compassion toward another living being. It extends itself beyond what anyone would expect an animal to be capable of. No one quite understands why; perhaps some animals have extra big hearts.

I will always remember a story I was told several years ago while paddling along the Zambezi River in Zimbabwe, Africa. Many dangers lurked in the hippo- and crocodile-infested waters, and our guides implored us to use extreme caution. "There is a crocodile every three meters [10 feet] throughout the river," the guides warned, "and they can grow up to six meters [20 feet] in length."

One of our guides, Washington, spoke about a group of tourists who had capsized their canoes on the Zambezi River. The group managed to find refuge on a sand island in the river, but the crocodiles were lurking nearby, and the guide felt he had no choice but to try to swim to the bank for help.

He almost made it to shore but was grabbed by a croc just few feet from the bank. The guide had the quick wits to ram his arm into the predator's deadly jaws. Located deep within the croc's throat is the epiglottal flap, which regulates the amount of water the reptile swallows. If the flap is kept open, the crocodile is forced to release its grip or it will drown.

The guide escaped and crawled up the bank, bloody and in shock, only to look into the eyes of a one-ton Cape buffalo—a notoriously dangerous, bad-tempered animal armed with a set of heavy, sharp horns. The guide must surely have thought he'd met his end. But the buffalo did not attack; instead, it stood guard over the guide's bleeding, weak body. The buffalo fended off crocodiles, hyenas and jackals throughout the night.

The next morning, the canoeists were saved when a search party spotted them from a helicopter. The guide was located, alive and lying on the shore next to the Cape buffalo. I asked Washington, "Why didn't the buffalo attack?"

Washington's reply was simple and made a strong impression on me. He said, "The buffalo was showing empathy for the injured animal." This beast had chosen to extend compassion to the guide and, in doing so, had saved his life.

What follows are stories that demonstrate an animal's intuition and sensitivity to life around it. These animals possessed the power to help heal and protect, and they affected the lives of other beings.

Walking Dreyfus

When Deb Proc's grandmother fell and broke her hip in 1996, it was a heartbreaking situation for the entire family. Her grandmother had been living an independent lifestyle up to that point, but she would now need to move into a nursing home. It was unbearable for Deb to see her normally jovial grandmother so upset. "She was devastated and wouldn't talk to anyone in the family, and when we came to visit her, she simply cried."

Desperate to find a way to help encourage her grandmother to talk, Deb asked one of the nurses at the Glenrose Rehabilitation Hospital, in Edmonton, Alberta, if she could bring her golden retriever, Dreyfus, for a visit. Her grandmother loved Deb's dog, so Deb hoped Dreyfus might be able to cheer her up. The nurse assured her that it would not be a problem, so on the next visit, Deb brought Dreyfus. "I put him on a chair beside the bed, and she turned to him and started to cry. She reached out to pet him and he gently nudged her, and through her tears, she started to laugh. She immediately started telling him how upset she was that she now had to count on others to take care of her."

The nurses were amazed. Not only was Deb's grandmother talking, but she was laughing too. Deb was delightfully shocked by her grandmother's positive reaction. Needless to say, Dreyfus continued to visit. Seeing firsthand the benefits that were derived from these visits, Deb and Dreyfus joined the Glenrose Rehabilitation Hospital's Pet Visitation Program a week later.

Dreyfus, now six years old, was a kind-hearted, loving chap. He and Deb had become regular faces at the Glenrose, visiting every Monday for Pet Visitation Night. Eager patients gathered in the common room, awaiting the arrival of their four-legged friends.

On one of their visits in 1997, they met a sweet, young girl named Samantha. The eight-year-old was seated in her wheelchair, looking sad. As soon as she laid eyes on Dreyfus, her face lit up. She gently reached out her hand to pet him, and he wagged his tail in return. Samantha had been in a serious car accident. She had been in a coma for more than three weeks, and when she finally awoke , she had no feeling on her left side or in her legs. Samantha was transferred to the Glenrose Rehabilitation Hospital for physiotherapy. The doctors warned her that even with intense therapy, she might never regain the use of her legs, and not to get her hopes up.

Samantha's mother was having a difficult time handling the prognosis. Visits from Dreyfus offered a small and welcome reprieve as she watched her daughter laugh and play with her new canine buddy. Dreyfus loved to visit all the patients, but he seemed to sense that Samantha needed him, and he always gravitated back to her.

After a few visits, Samantha said during a visitation, "I'm going to work very hard in physio, and when I can walk on my own, would you let me take Dreyfus all by myself?"

Deb, not knowing how serious her injury was, replied, "Of course you can walk him by yourself—you just tell me when you're ready and I'll hand you the leash."

Samantha started her therapy the following week; it was hard, painful work. The weeks progressed, and one day Samantha' mother told Deb, "All Sam talks about every day is that she has to work harder so that she can walk Dreyfus by herself. She is very focused and refuses to give up." Deb worried that perhaps she had given Samantha an unrealistic goal.

Months passed, and Deb and Dreyfus continued to visit the patients every week. Each visit was particularly meaningful for the brave little girl. Samantha told Dreyfus all about her rehab that week, and Dreyfus responded by snuggling up, licking her hand and doing silly tricks to make her laugh. Like a children's clown, Dreyfus had a large bag of tricks, and he could roll over, play dead or wave, much to the delight of his audience.

"It was very heartwarming to see Dreyfus communicate with Sam. I am always amazed by the sensitivity of our pets and how they seem to know and sense what people need. Dreyfus seemed to know when she just needed a hug, when she needed to smile and even when she needed to play."

One night, Deb and Dreyfus arrived for their regular visit. The room was full of patients, and Samantha was waiting in her regular spot, wearing an extra big grin. As they approached,

Samantha and Dreyfus share a smiling moment together.

~❦~

Samantha took a deep breath and ever so slowly stood up. The room went silent, and then everyone burst into loud applause. Dreyfus ran up to greet her and tried to lick her face. Even he seemed to know that a miracle had just taken place. Tears filled Samantha's mother's eyes as she reminded Deb of Samantha's goal to one day walk Dreyfus all by herself. A dream that once seemed impossibly out of reach had just inched a little closer to home.

Two months later, at Pet Visitation Night, Samantha wasn't sitting in her usual spot. Deb turned to look for her, and Dreyfus seemed confused as he scanned the room for his favorite buddy. A moment later, Samantha proudly entered the room, with slow tentative steps and the help of a cane. Deb stood in shock. There was only one thing to do. Says Deb, "I handed her the leash!"

Samantha was beaming and reached down to gently pet Dreyfus. "You helped me to walk again. I couldn't have done this without you. You are the best dog ever!" Dreyfus had unwittingly become the incentive that helped motivate Samantha through five arduous, pain-filled months of physiotherapy.

Samantha and her mom returned to their home in Fort McMurray, Alberta. Deb kept in touch over the years. This was truly an experience she would never forget. "I can't think of anything I do that I get more instant rewards and appreciation for, by simply giving an hour of my time. The patients I visit literally light up—not because of me, but because of my golden buddy! I get pet therapy every day when I go home, so I think it's only fair that I share! Just watching the patients with him is like getting a very special present every week."

When Samantha was older, she started volunteering at the local hospital. Dreyfus was an excellent role model for volunteerism, and she wanted to help other people just like Dreyfus had helped her. Eleven years after her accident, Samantha's goal remained the same—to help others. She was preparing for a career in social work as well as working at certifying one of her two goldens, Molly, as a therapy dog.

To this day, photos of Dreyfus hang on the walls of Samantha's bedroom so that she will never forget how he helped her. Even though she now has her own golden retrievers to walk, she will always carry Dreyfus in her heart.

Creature Feature

The healing benefit of using animals to help in the medical treatment of humans was first mentioned in 460 BC. Hippocrates wrote about the benefits of riding a horse to rehabilitate an injury. Today, Hippotheraphy (*hippo* is Greek for "horse") is a used for therapeutic purposes throughout North America and Europe.

Follow Me

Few animals can match the whimsical charm and appeal of dolphins. They seem to always wear a smile and are loved for their gentle, playful nature. Most biologists believe dolphins are intelligent creatures. Their complex language—a system of whistles, squeaks and clicks—has been the focus of many scientific studies in the hopes that one day, humans might understand and even communicate with these enchanting animals.

Dolphins are revered by many cultures, and their mystical powers are spoken of in legends.

These myths are thought to have originated in Greece. A Greek coin featuring a boy riding on the back of a dolphin dates back to 272 BC. The Maori people of New Zealand consider dolphins to be *Kaitiaki* or guardians, protectors of our souls, and their myths tell of dolphins saving people lost at sea. Today, there are many accounts of surfers being protected by dolphins from an attacking shark, so it seems these stories are rooted in reality.

Pelorus Jack was a famous dolphin that helped guide ships safely across New Zealand's Cook Strait, a dangerous stretch of water with submerged rocks and fast currents. The dolphin was first noticed in 1888, and for the next 24 years, he faithfully met boats to ride their bow waves and escort them through the treacherous waters. Pelorus Jack's role in preventing shipwrecks and saving lives was so valued that he was the first dolphin in the world to be protected by law.

Dolphins have become well known for their altruistic activities through the ages, so it shouldn't have come as a surprise when a New Zealand bottlenose dolphin saved the lives of two whales. But those who witnessed the act were left completely speechless.

The New Zealand Department of Conservation was called out March 10, 2008, to see if they could help a 10-foot mother pygmy sperm whale and her male calf. The pair was beached on a sandbar just off Mahia Beach, northeast of Wellington.

Volunteers tried four times to reorient them in the right direction, but the whales were confused and repeatedly became stranded. They could not seem to find their way past the sandbar to open water.

Rescue workers kept at it for over an hour and a half until the workers and whales were exhausted. It did not look promising for the whales; the next step was to have the veterinarian euthanize the mammals to prevent a prolonged death.

The marine mammals were showing signs of distress. Fortunately, the playful Mahia Beach dolphin named Moko by local residents arrived on the scene. Moko had become a regular at the beach, engaging with the swimmers and pushing kayakers, to their delight. This time however, Moko was on a mission.

Moko swam up to the beached whales and appeared to communicate with them. The whales responded, and within minutes, they followed Moko almost 200 yards along the shoreline to the edge of the sandbar, before turning right to swim through a narrow channel out to open sea.

The quick-thinking dolphin came to the rescue and deliberately guided the two whales to safety. The feat was nothing short of amazing to the rescuers and local marine mammals experts.

Conservation Officer Malcolm Smith told *The Daily Telegraph*, "The whales were...quite distressed. They had arched their backs and were calling to one another, but as soon as the dolphin turned up, they submerged into the water and followed her."

"Moko just came flying through the water and pushed in between us and the whales," Juanita Symes, one of the rescuers, reported to the Associated Press.

There is no evidence that bottlenose dolphins speak the same language as pygmy sperm whales, but to those that watched, there was no doubt that they were communicating with each other. It is possible that Moko was drawn to the area because she heard the whale's distress calls. The whales have not been seen since; with Moko's help, they found their way to freedom. Malcolm Smith told *National Geographic*, "This is the first recorded instance of something like this happening." What a fantastic event to witness.

After leading the two cetaceans to sea, the hero dolphin returned to the beach to play and splash about with the humans. Moko's helping hand, or rather flipper, was truly a miracle of nature.

Watch Over Me

So many events in nature remain mysteries, and as hard as science toils to apply logic and reason to explain all things, life continues to unfold in curious ways. Take, for example, the perplexing incident that occurred in the remote region of Bita Genet, Ethiopia, in June 2005.

Seven men abducted a 12-year-old village girl in the hopes of forcing her to marry one of them. As inconceivable as it seems, kidnapping young girls is part of the "marriage custom" in rural areas; the United Nations estimates that over 70 percent of all marriages in Ethiopia are by abduction.

The men held the child against her will for a week, beating her repeatedly in an attempt to get her to submit to marriage. The youngster was eventually rescued when three lions happened upon the group and chased the men away. Expecting an attack from the lions, which would be normal under the circumstances, the men fled for their lives, forgetting about the young girl.

The girl was crying, terrified from the ordeal and covered with cuts and bruises from the abuse. The pride of black-maned lions, however, did not attack the girl; instead, they protected her until the police and members of her family found her, half a day later. Sergeant Wondimu Wedajo told the Associated Press, "They stood guard until we found her, and then they just left her like a gift and went back into the forest."

The police were able to catch four of the seven offenders. Although no one will ever know for sure why the lions chose not to attack the girl, one thing is certain—they saved her from further torment and violence by her captors.

One wildlife expert speculated that the lions did not eat the girl because she was whimpering, a sound much like the mewing sound of a lion cub. But perhaps these majestic members of the animal kingdom were simply watching over the vulnerable, frightened child, guarding her from further harm. The wonders of nature never cease to amaze.

Creature Feature

Ethiopia's lions—famous for their thick, black manes—are the country's national symbol and appear on its currency. It is estimated that only 1000 of these rare lions remain in the wild.

Acts of Kindness

The expression "pay it forward" describes the action of repaying a good deed you have received by doing something kind for others. It was coined by an Ohio State University football coach by the name of Wayne Woodrow "Woody" Hayes. Hayes was well known for winning scores of national titles and championships, *and* for his famous quotes, including "You can never pay back, but you can always pay forward."

One wouldn't think that a member of the animal world could act on the concept, but a kind-hearted greyhound has done just that. Malnourished, abused and caked in dirt, an abandoned greyhound left to die in a shed was rescued in 2003 and nursed back to health. The dog was fortunate to have been saved and has returned the good deed by paying the love forward to others...50 times!

Police in Warwickshire, England, discovered the greyhound, whimpering and frightened, locked in a garden shed. The police took the female dog to Geoff Grewcock at the Nuneaton Warwickshire Wildlife Sanctuary. Geoff had originally set up the sanctuary to care for sick and injured wildlife, but over the years he began to accept pets that were dumped or mistreated by their not-so-loving owners.

After several weeks of care and interaction, Geoff and his staff nursed the dog back to health and earned her trust. They named the pretty gal Jasmine and were searching for an adoptive home for her when she took on the role of "meeter and greeter" at the sanctuary.

Jasmine was the first to welcome any new animal that arrived; whether it was an orphaned or abandoned fox cub, rabbit or baby bird, she peeked eagerly into the box or cage, her soft, doe-like eyes inspecting her new charge, before delivering a loving lick. Geoff shares one of Jasmine's motherly moments on the Wildlife Sanctuary website:

We had two puppies that had been abandoned by a nearby railway line. They were tiny when they arrived at the center, and Jasmine approached them and grabbed one by the scruff of the neck in her mouth and put him on the settee. Then she fetched the other one and sat down with them, cuddling them.

Jasmine is like this with all the animals: she licks the rabbits and guinea pigs, cuddles the fox and badger cubs and patiently allows birds to perch on the bridge of her nose. This forsaken creature, once timid and fearful from a past of ill treatment, has become a surrogate mother to all those in need of her attention. She is able to calm the animals and help them settle into their new environment. Geoff says, "She simply dotes on the animals as if they were her own. It's incredible to see."

This extraordinary rescue dog seems to have moved beyond her history of neglect and showers warmth and affection to all in need. Her maternal instincts are abundant and are paired with a big heart; she has cared for dozens of orphaned and abandoned critters: five fox cubs, four badger cubs, 15 chicks, eight guinea pigs, two stray puppies and 15 rabbits.

In December 2008, five years after Jasmine was rescued from certain death, she became a surrogate mother for the 50th time—this time to a tiny 11-week-old roe deer fawn. A dog walker found the fawn, named Bramble, semi-conscious in a field. She was brought to the sanctuary, where seven-year-old Jasmine immediately jumped in with all four legs and a tail, cuddling up with the fawn to keep it warm.

The two have become inseparable, and they walk around the sanctuary exchanging kisses. Bramble walks between the long, slender legs of the greyhound and Jasmine checks Bramble's fur, removing matted bits and debris.

With the compassion and empathy of a doting mom, Jasmine has eased the stress of 50 frightened and lonely babies and youngsters. She doesn't care what they look like or if they hop, fly or run. What is important to this dear girl is extending kindness to everyone she meets.

CHAPTER SIX

Animal Crackers

All of the animals except for man know that the principle business of life is to enjoy it.

—Samuel Butler

ANIMALS ARE UTTERLY CAPTIVATING to watch. Even when they're not trying, they'll upstage a human any day. No wonder there are so many television programs about animals and shows that showcase their funniest and zaniest moments.

The joy of animals is that you never quite know just what they will do or when they will do it. My mother remembers working in the show ring with Duke, our first family dog. He was a gorgeous German shepherd and was supremely well behaved in the ring.

Duke was a brainy dog, and he knew his commands. Not only had he rescued me when, as a toddler, I escaped from the yard and was bee-lining it for the wooded ravine and river, but he had apprehended burglars in our home on two separate occasions. Duke was amazing, and he had a stack of ribbons and awards to prove it.

On one particular evening Duke, known as Duke of Dafay in the ring, won the "Best Canadian Bred in a Group" award. My mom, pregnant with me at the time, stood in the ring with her prized pooch beside her and the winning ribbon in her hand. Unbeknownst to my mother, my dad had joined the audience and was sitting in the sixth row of the bleachers. He had been out of town on business and had decided to stop by and surprise her.

Somehow, Duke spotted dad in the bleachers and took off like a shot. He charged across the ring and leaped over a six-foot fence into the audience. He was extremely excited to see my dad and, apparently, needed to let him know at that precise moment.

My mother was mortified as she stood in the ring clutching his winning ribbon for good behavior. Like I said, you never quite know what animals are going to do.

There's a Mouse in My Trunk

There is a funny scene in Disney's famous film *Dumbo* in which little Timothy Q. Mouse has some giant elephants quivering in terror. Seems ridiculous that a huge animal could be afraid of a wee mouse, but that rumor has been around for ages.

Some people speculate that elephants are scared of a mouse crawling into the end of their trunk and plugging it up so they can't breathe. Of course, one could ask, why would a mouse want to travel up an elephant's trunk?

In my exhaustive research on the matter, I could not find one single documented incident in which a mouse ended up in an elephant's trunk...well, that is, until I spoke to Maureen Anderson at the Edmonton Valley Zoo in Alberta.

Maureen has worked with many animals throughout her 24 years at the zoo, but her favorite resident is a loving, 9000-pound Asian elephant named Lucy. They share a tremendous bond. Maureen has been a steady companion for more than two decades and, along with the other elephant keepers, is part of Lucy's family.

Like all elephants, Lucy is intelligent and enjoys new challenges and activities that keep her busy. She's fond of long walks through the trees behind the zoo, and she has a flare for abstract art. In fact, she paints dynamic abstracts, carefully choosing her colors and brushes to create just the right look. She is Canada's most famous pachyderm painter; her work is featured in several art shows and it sells well.

Lucy is truly an exceptional gal, especially when it comes to games. Her favorite pastime is playing hide-and-seek with Maureen. All right, it's a little tricky for Lucy to hide with her size and all, but she loves trying to discover Maureen's hiding spots.

Back in 1993, Lucy and Maureen were playing hide-and-seek in the old elephant building. There was a large bathing pool with walkways enclosed by walls running along the sides. Maureen would run back and forth behind the walls, where Lucy couldn't see her but, with her sensitive trunk, could *smell* her.

Maureen was quietly tucked behind one of the walls as Lucy's eight-foot-long trunk sniffed slowly along the ground, feeling for her keeper. Just then, Maureen noticed a tiny mouse hightailing it down the hall, heading in the direction of Lucy's trunk.

She couldn't believe her eyes or the timing. This mouse was clearly out to set a new rodent record for the 50-meter sprint. As Lucy continued waving her trunk along the floor, sniffing and breathing in the air in search of Maureen, she inhaled the mouse right up her trunk like a vacuum cleaner.

Before Maureen could react, Lucy fired out the mouse, like a ball shooting out of a cannon. The mouse rocketed from Lucy's trunk, which was still resting on the floor, and skidded to a halt 20 feet away. It stood up and ran in the opposite direction, never to be seen again.

In the end, once she cleared her airway, Lucy was ready for another round of hide-and-seek; the mouse, judging by the speed with which it raced

Maureen watches as Lucy paints one of her famous abstracts.

away, was fine; and Maureen was gifted with a great memory to laugh at every now and again. Lucy and the mouse: a funny story with a happy ending courtesy of the world's greatest natural comedians—members of the animal kingdom.

Although animals can be natural jokers and tricksters, sometimes their comedic timing isn't appreciated until *after* the fact, as in this next story....

Nerves of Steel

Doug Steele has worked under challenging circumstances and has endured extreme conditions, all in the pursuit of filming wildlife. Projects have taken this award-winning cinematographer to Africa, Australia, Central America and North America, where he has filmed on land and underwater since 1985.

Animals are especially tricky to film; they are unpredictable, don't adhere to a schedule and can be dangerous. Getting the shot can often be hit or miss. However, Doug discovered that, with creative ingenuity and a great deal of patience, it was usually possible to get the shot you hoped for. It may take hours, even days, and require several attempts, but if you were persistent, you would be rewarded.

Doug was still relatively new to wildlife filmmaking in the spring of 1987 when he started filming black bears for a one-hour documentary entitled *World of the Wily Black Bear*, by Karvonen Films. Doug's goal was to capture a variety of black bear behaviors on film: peeling bark off a tree to feed on insects and sap, a sow nursing cubs and catching salmon, to name a few.

This was Doug's first bear film, so he was learning how to "read" the animal and sense its next move. He was filming black bears across Alberta and British Columbia, following up on reported sightings. Through trial and error, he was learning how to set up situations to get the shot in the most time- and energy-efficient way. He never knew until he tried how something was actually going to turn out.

One of the things he'd learned was to create a scent trail with dead fish or a moose hide. The bear usually sniffed the ground and followed the trail. So, if you positioned your camera just right, hiding behind a blind if necessary, you were likely to get your shot.

All wildlife cinematographers and directors ask pretty much the same questions: What kind of footage am I going to get? How much danger will I be in? What's going to happen? One can never predict exactly what an animal is going to do.

Doug was after a den sequence and desperately wanted a shot of a black bear entering the den, taken from the inside. He had no intention of sharing the den with the bear, so he had to ask himself how he could get the shot. It would be tricky to pull off, but Doug felt the impact in the finished film would be worth the effort.

He had been filming a gorgeous juvenile black bear around Amisk Lake in central Alberta and had noticed an old den. Doug investigated the den and pondered how he could set things up to get his shot.

The den was located on the side of a sandy hill and tunneled five or six feet into the slope. He circled around the den to the back end and dug down about four feet. Scraping away the sand, he created a small opening about nine inches in diameter in the back wall of the den, the right size to accommodate his camera lens. He fitted the hole with a piece of glass so the bear wouldn't pick up his scent.

Now he needed to create a safety barrier between him and the bear. Using a piece of plywood and a few logs, he assembled a rather primitive setup so a lid could cover the hole once he was settled inside. Next, he needed to give the bear incentive to enter the den.

Doug found a beaver carcass near the lake. He sealed it in a drum and set it in the sun to rot for a few days. Then he dragged the carcass through the valley, up a path toward the den and through the opening, leaving a few bits of meat in the center of the chamber.

Finally, he positioned the camera so that when the time came, he was ready to roll. Light peeked through the sides of the lid, so Doug could focus and adjust his settings as needed. Now, the hard part: waiting for the bear to show up. It would be day two before Doug was graced with his furry star's presence.

Doug was in place by daylight, comfortably perched on the hill. His hiding area was right next to him, so it would be easy to hop down, drag the plywood lid in place and get into position to film. He pulled out his book and started to read to pass the hours. It was a pleasant and relaxing scene; the sun was warm, birds were chirping and he had packed a lunch to nibble on. All was well.

He waited, confident that the bear would not creep up behind him but would follow the scent trail he had carefully laid down, allowing Doug ample time to scramble quietly into the hole without being spotted. The day passed leisurely.

At 4:00 PM, he caught sight of the black bear, sniffing the ground and ambling his way toward the den. Doug's tranquility was replaced with a surge of adrenaline. His heart was thumping and he could feel himself starting to sweat as he quickly lowered himself into the hole and slid the makeshift lid over top. His hands were a little shaky with the excitement, but he was ready to capture the winning shot. He waited, barely breathing with anticipation.

Doug could see the tip of the bear's nose through the lens and thought, "Here he comes. Oh, this is great!" But then…the bear was gone. Doug had no idea where he went or what had happened. He waited to see if the bear would come back into view. That's when everything went dark and sand started to fall behind his head.

The black bear had decided to park his 200-pound frame on top of the lid, directly over Doug's head. The bear sat there for a while, sniffing the area. He had caught a whiff of some *fresh* smells and was curious. Bears are extremely inquisitive and tend to meticulously investigate anything new. Doug had no choice but to sit tight, be quiet and wait.

The bear sat there for what felt like an eternity. What was he doing, admiring the scenery? Doug's mind was racing, and he feared that his ramshackle structure would collapse and he would be crushed.

Finally, the black bear lifted his big rump from the lid and wandered around to the other side, entering the den to snack on the carcass morsels. Mission accomplished! Doug got it all on film.

He mopped the sweat from his brow, pleased to have nailed the shot. His parting thoughts were, "That was a lot of work for a seven-second shot, but definitely worth it."

Moose Mania

When Cyndi Ardiel peeked out her kitchen window one spring day in 1997 to check on her one-year-old colt, Ebenezer, she couldn't believe her eyes. There was Ebenezer, gaily running around his pen, chasing a young female moose.

Cyndi raced outside to make sure her eyes weren't playing tricks on her, and she confirmed the incredible sight, except now the moose was chasing the colt. After a few laps, the duo stopped to catch their breath, and then tag-you're-it started up again. She called her husband, the kids and her neighbors; they had to see this to believe it.

Cyndi checked the fence enclosing the five-acre horse pen to see how the moose got in. The area was a combination of pasture, bush and trees. She couldn't see any breaks in the fence so assumed the moose must have jumped over it.

The family owned 33 acres of land in the hamlet of Wharncliffe, in northeastern Ontario. They had a mare and her colt, Ebenezer, as well as a dog and a rabbit. Cyndi had noticed earlier in the day that the mare was acting nervous and giving off loud snorts. Finally, she saw the mare bolt for the barn, which was her safe place to go whenever something bothered her.

This particular mare was afraid of simply everything, including the red brick walkway that ran next to the house. When she was ridden, she went to great lengths to avoid the "evil" walkway. Like most horses, she was wary and cautious of new things and other animals. Horses evolved as prey animals, so their first response to anything frightening is flight. This mare, in particular, was always tentative.

Cyndi scanned the area but didn't see anything that could have spooked the horse. Nevertheless, she locked the mare in the barn and let Ebenezer out for some pasture time. Ebby, as the family had nicknamed him, did not have the usual cautious horse personality. He was spirited, outgoing and absolutely fearless. The colt tossed caution out the barn door and chased cats, dogs, crows, ravens and even wolves. In fact, he was a proficient mouser. He did not appreciate other animals venturing into *his* field or barn. His registered name, "Spirit's Taken By Storm," was oddly fitting.

But for some reason, Ebby had given the thumbs-up to the young moose. Cyndi estimated the calf to be about two years of age. Calves generally stay with their mother for at least a year after birth.

Once the mother calves again the following spring, she drives her yearlings off. No doubt this is a difficult transition for a calf, so perhaps this young female was lonely for some company.

The colt and the moose calf were almost identical in size, each with long, slim legs, perfect for a game of tag. Cyndi remembers, "They would take turns chasing each other. Then one would stop, and they would stand close to each other. All of a sudden, the one being chased would spin around and pursue the other."

The romp went on all day until Cyndi put Ebby into the barn for the night. She assumed the moose would leave the way she had entered and by morning would be gone. But the next morning, there was the moose, patiently waiting in the pasture for Ebby.

Cyndi let Ebby out of the barn to see what would happen. The two spindly-legged youngsters took up where they left off, and the game was on. Word was spreading around the area: "Have you heard about the horse and the moose that play tag?" Soon, folks were traveling from all over to see the show and take pictures or catch the antics on video.

The moose did not appear to mind the attention as crowds gathered to watch and smile. She grazed on birch and poplar leaves and twigs, and drank water from the horse barrel. The field was flanked by bush, so at night there were many places for the moose to curl up and sleep.

By day five, it appeared that this moose had no intention of leaving. Cyndi put Ebby to bed in the barn that night and decided to leave the gate open just in case the moose wanted to leave. The next morning, the pasture was vacant; Ebby's playmate had gone back into the bush, probably missing her diet of water plants from the nearby lakes and marshes.

Cyndi and her family still laugh when they remember Ebenezer and the gangly young moose frolicking in the pasture. Who knows why these two unlikely animals decided to become buddies? Maybe Ebenezer was happy to have finally met someone his own size. Perhaps the calf needed a little companionship before adjusting to a world without his mom. Either way, it put smiles on a lot of faces.

Creature Feature

Moose are the world's largest deer. They can run 35 miles per hour and swim for 10 miles. A male's antlers can spread six feet from end to end. A male can use his antlers to battle a predator, and both males and females can destroy an attacker by kicking with their sharp hooves.

Hoo Are You Looking At?

One chilly winter day in 2009, a great horned owl bit off a little more than it could chew. The large owl, showing off a wing span of almost four feet, swooped down to take a little teacup Maltese named Mattie from her backyard. Mattie was out for some fresh air and to do her morning "business" when the raptor swooped down and grabbed the five-pound pooch with its curved talons.

Luckily, Mattie was a bit too big for the owl to lift off the ground. The dog's owner, Carrie Lyle, was in the kitchen when she heard the commotion and raced outside to help her dog. The owl flew off and perched on the roof but continued to eye the dog with interest.

This appeared to be a determined owl with an agenda, but something wasn't quite right. These birds of prey are indeed meat eaters, but they usually hunt mice, rabbits, birds and large insects. As well, they characteristically begin to hunt at dusk, not first thing in the morning.

Carrie called Hardy Pletz, a master bird bander, to see if he could help. Hardy had handled thousands of Alberta's wild birds over the years while banding. He was an expert at identifying the birds' species, age and sex, and understood their particular behaviors and traits.

Once Hardy saw the great horned owl, he knew exactly what the problem was. The female owl was severely emaciated and desperate for food. Great horned owls are the largest of all "eared" owls, measuring up to 25 inches in length and weighing over four pounds. They require a steady diet of flesh to maintain their weight.

Hardy enticed the hungry owl down off the roof with a dead mouse, and when she went to take the prey, he swiftly caught her with his net and took her to the Wildlife Rehabilitation Society of Edmonton for treatment.

This beautiful speckled owl with her prominent ear tufts (the horns) was thin and would not have lasted much longer without food. The staff and volunteers needed to increase her body weight and rehydrate her. They began to tube feed the owl immediately.

It was important to monitor her progress, so she was weighed daily. The owl was kept in a large enclosure to recover and had minimal contact with her caretakers so she would not become habituated to humans. They needed her to stay wild so she would survive once they released her. This gal was as feisty as they come and was vocal about her captive situation.

Within a couple weeks, she reached a healthy body weight and was transferred to the outdoor flight pen. The larger enclosure was an ideal place for her to get used to the winter weather and practice flying before being released.

Three days after the owl was transferred into her flight pen, one of the wildlife rehabilitators went outside to feed her and change her water. The pen appeared to be empty. The worker looked from corner to corner and searched high and low, but there was no sign of the owl.

Then she caught movement out of the corner of her eye. This wise bird, holding true to the owl's intelligent reputation, had figured out a way to "wiggle between the mesh on the top of the flight pen and the boards." Before the animal caretaker could grab a ladder to seal the area, the owl had "released" herself and was perched on a telephone pole close by, looking down smugly with her large, round, gold eyes.

This "hoo-dini" was clearly well enough to be free but had escaped before being banded, a routine procedure for all birds at the shelter. Banding helps to track the lives of the birds once they are released and monitors their progress as they migrate and set up territories throughout North America. Would the owl go back to her original territory, which backed onto a large treed park, or would she seek out a new dog-free area?

Within three weeks, Hardy came to the shelter exclaiming, "You are not going to believe this, but I got a call from the people living next door to the Maltese, and the great horned owl is back watching the dog!" The owl would come to visit first thing in the morning and again at dusk, perching on the roof of Mattie's house and giving the dog "owly" looks.

Great horned owl with an owly glare

Now that Hardy knew where the owl was living, he was eager to band her. She had already flown the coop on him once before. When he spotted the owl, he was pleased to see that her weight was good, so her fixation on Mattie was not because she was starving.

Once again, he enticed the owl down off the roof with a dead mouse and skillfully caught her with his net. This time, the spirited owl was in healthy condition and immediately freaked out and started hooting at him. It was as if she was yelling, "Hey, I remember *you*, and I am not going back to that rehabilitation place filled with humans!" Hardy was pleased to see her spunk and banded her quickly before letting her go.

To this day, the great horned owl and Mattie share the same territory, but it seems both are wiser for the experience and keep one eye focused on the other. Mattie surveys the yard thoroughly before setting out, and the owl knows if she tries any funny business with the dog again, Hardy and his net will be back.

Section Three

Kindred Spirits

Who can believe that there is no soul
behind those luminous eyes!

−Theophile Gautier

We humans tend to journey through life in search of a kindred spirit—someone we can bond with, who feels and thinks the way we do and who is similar in temperament and nature. Quite simply, we seek to connect with another being, one with whom we have something in common.

These bonds are few and far between, which makes them all the more special when they happen. I believe that kindred spirits share a rare spiritual link, a connection that you can't quite explain. There are so many mysteries in nature that cannot be explained, that defy common sense, logic and science. These magical events open our minds, change our perspectives and allow our thinking to evolve outside the accepted boundaries. Perhaps, for example, an animal can have a kindred spirit. Why not? Or a human might find a deep kinship with an animal. Certainly, we accept a dog as "man's best friend," a common human-animal bond we see in everyday life.

There are many stories of animals that have formed inter-species bonds, bonds that cross the lines of what is perceived as "normal" behavior. Folklore and mythology are rich with stories that describe extraordinary encounters between animals, as well as with the human animal.

The founding of Rome, for example, is embroiled in myth. The legend tells us that twin brothers, Romulus and Remus, were found and suckled by a she-wolf. The brothers later founded the great city of Rome in 753 BC. And the Bible talks about the prophet Elijah, hiding in the wilderness near a brook as God had directed him to. Each morning and evening the ravens cared for him, bringing bread and flesh to keep him alive.

Cartoon characters, such as Bugs Bunny, taught us as kids that a "wascally wabbit," Porky Pig, Sylvester the Cat and Wile E. Coyote could all co-exist. The rules for who was a predator and who was prey were blurred in lieu of entertainment and some laughs. There were many feuds and conflicts along the way, but in the end, it worked out okay, and nobody ate anybody else.

Walt Disney was the king of pairing unlikely critters. Bambi, the fawn, grew up with his friends—Thumper, the rabbit, and Flower, the skunk. Nobody thought twice about whether these accounts were true or not; they were just good stories.

In October 2005 at Tokyo's Mutsugoro Okoku Zoo, zookeepers were flabbergasted when they presented a 3.5-inch dwarf hamster to a three-foot-long rat snake, and the two became buddies. The rat snake had been refusing to eat its usual diet of frozen mice. The zookeepers were getting worried about his "hunger strike" and decided to offer a hamster, hoping that it would stimulate the snake's appetite. Instead, the two became friends. They huddled together in their heated cage, and the hamster even climbed on top of the snake's coiled body to nap. Talk about erasing the divide between predator and prey.

As it turns out, creatures of different species really do form unusual and unlikely bonds. There are many reasons why they connect; often it stems from survival or a desire for companionship. Interspecies bonds are often surprising, sometimes shocking and always endearing. They remind us that we don't understand everything that goes on in the animal kingdom. There are still plenty of surprises for us to discover and much for us to learn.

We marvel at these stories and ponder, "How is that possible?" In a world full of discord and unrest that stems from differences of opinion, appearance, behavior and belief, these stories offer hope. They suggest that perhaps we could all try a little harder to get along. Perhaps these stories will nudge you to look at your relationships, with both humans and other animals, with new eyes. Your kindred spirit just may be nearby.

CHAPTER SEVEN

Foster Moms

Animals are reliable, many full of love, true in their affections, predictable in their actions, grateful and loyal. Difficult standards for people to live up to.

—Alfred A. Montapert

WHAT IS CUTER THAN a baby? Absolutely nothing! And whether you are admiring the two- or four-legged animal, they typically share the same "baby-type" face: large, wide-set eyes, a small nose and features confined to the lower half of the face, making their forehead appear large and bulbous and their head round and symmetrical.

There is a reason that all babies have these features, and evolutionary psychologists sum it up like this: human babies, along with many animal newborns, are relatively helpless at birth and depend on others to look after them. So, it is in the infant's best interest to have features that attract others of that species. It is an evolutionary mechanism, a kind of insurance that guarantees the baby will be cared for. Apparently, large eyes and round heads are nature's way of making the baby adorable and irresistible, ensuring that the family and community keep an eye on the babe.

In complex societies, like those of whales, elephants and primates, surrogate females help to raise and teach the infant as it grows up. Extended family members stick around to keep an eye on junior.

However, life in the animal kingdom can be harsh, and babies are sometimes orphaned because the mother dies or rejects them. These infants face serious challenges, and the odds of survival are usually against them. Starvation, dehydration, predation and exposure to the elements are all harsh realities that face a lone creature separated prematurely from its mother.

Sometimes, however, a mother from a completely different species steps in and takes charge. It may look odd and appear somewhat awkward, but the mother carries on with her usual tasks of nursing, washing, protecting and playing with the newcomer as if it were one of her own. Her natural instincts take over, and she is in baby love. Isn't it wonderful that biological differences can be shelved and motherhood can cross species lines?

Squirrelly Situation

Mother Nature's magic appears in wonderful, and often surprising, ways. She shows us that sometimes when one door closes, another opens, and that even the most tumultuous beginning can have a happy ending.

This was the case for a baby squirrel, eyes not yet opened and utterly alone in the world. The orphan was found at the base of a tree in Renton, Washington, a suburb situated 13 miles southeast of Seattle. A woman found the infant squirrel lying on the ground along with his dead mother and sister. They had fallen 40 feet out of their nest. The mother may have been the unintended victim of rat poison carelessly left out. It appeared that the little one miraculously survived because he had landed on his mother.

On September 9, 2005, Debby Cantlon received a call about the baby squirrel. Debby, well known in the Seattle area for nursing injured and sick animals back to health, agreed to take in the squirrel to see what she could do for him. Now this may seem like an unusual request, but friends and strangers had been bringing injured animals to Debby for as long as she could remember.

Animals were the love of her life and she had a knack for saving them, but this baby squirrel was so young, and on top of being injured, was also malnourished and severely dehydrated. Caring for the newborn squirrel demanded round-the-clock attention, but Debby didn't think twice. Having lived with cancer the last two years, Debby found helping animals therapeutic.

She named the tiny critter Finnegan and set about preparing a warm, snuggly nest in a cage where he could recover. She added a heat source and began the tasks of bottle-feeding and rehabilitation. She knew that little Finnegan had a fight ahead of him and that it would be touch and go for the newborn squirrel.

What happened next was a surprise—one of Mother Nature's tender strokes that caught the attention of several newspapers and broadcasters. The family dog, a sable and white papillon named Mademoiselle Giselle, dragged Finnegan's cage clear across the house, planting it right next to her doggie bed. The pregnant pooch had shown a lot of interest in Finnegan since he had arrived. Of course, one couldn't be sure if it was maternal instinct kicking in or if she was hoping for a tasty snack! At any rate, this deliberate squirrel-napping occurred twice before the night she delivered her pups.

As Debby told CBS's *The Early Show*, "The next morning, I saw that she was paying more attention to the squirrel than she was to her own puppies. She was feeling terribly torn. It was like half of her babies were in one place, and the rest were in another place." Debby wrestled with the decision to open the cage and let Mademoiselle Giselle meet Finnegan face to face. She was concerned that her dog might accidentally harm the little squirrel. But she finally opened the cage door, and the introduction was an instant success.

Finnegan the squirrel joins his litter mates for breakfast
courtesy of Mademoiselle Giselle.

Mama Giselle was ecstatic and immediately
started licking and nuzzling the squirrel as if
he was her own. Her instinct took over in his
time of need, and it didn't matter a bit that she
was a dog and he was a squirrel. The interspecies
bonding had begun, and Finnegan was officially
adopted. A journey of healing and love for
a wee squirrel, a dog and an animal lover was
about to unfold.

Debby continued to bottle-feed the squirrel.
Mademoiselle Giselle became a willing aide,
allowing Finnegan to burrow in and nurse alongside her five puppies, then just two days old. She
actually encouraged him to suckle with the others,

after which he'd curl up to his new siblings and settle in for a cozy nap. Finnegan was at home.

His siblings enjoyed his company, too, and were always happy to see him. They all played together, crawling over each other's furry bodies and pressing their noses up to his. What a sight—five squirming puppies and one squirrel piled on top of each other as a doting papillon, with long-haired butterfly ears, affectionately watched over them. There is no doubt that the interspecies bonding helped Finnegan become healthy and recover from his ordeal.

By the time Finnegan was six weeks old, he had grown into a strong and curious guy, climbing and exploring at ease, while the pups were still barely walking. Debby began to wean Finnegan and feed him only with a bottle, preparing him for his eventual release back into the wild. She knew that squirrels should not be kept as pets, so the next step was to teach Finnegan how to forage for food by himself and get some practice cracking nuts and seeds.

Debby recalls, "I gradually cut back the bottled milk and would hold a bowl of nuts and sunflower seeds in my hand for him to nibble on. At first he wasn't at all interested, but then he started to get the hang of it. One day he grabbed a peanut and then took off to hide it."

When Finnegan reached eight weeks, Debby felt it was the right time for him to become acquainted with the outdoors. She remembers, "He would run around freely but would not go beyond the edge of the yard, and every night he would scratch at the back door or window for me to let him in."

One night, he didn't come back. It would be two weeks before he returned for a brief visit. Then he disappeared again and returned in spring. It appeared that Finnegan had found a mate and was building a nest. "He came close, but he wouldn't let me touch him," Debby told the *Seattle Times*. "He just wanted me to know he was OK. He's wild and free and happy, and doing exactly what he's supposed to be doing."

And so the life of a tiny, orphaned squirrel was saved by a big-hearted woman committed to help-ing animals and by the actions of a loving dog, willing to overlook a few differences and accept the bushy-tailed creature as one of her own.

Creature Feature

There are more than 300 species of squirrels worldwide. This group of rodents includes the tree squirrel, ground squirrel and flying squirrel. Squirrels' teeth grow continuously. Their incisors grow six inches per year, so the squirrels must chew constantly on branches to keep them short.

Golden Girl

Tom and Allie Harvey own and operate the Safari Zoological Park in Caney, Kansas. The park is home to a collection of exotic cats including tigers, lions, a black leopard and a jaguar, as well as grizzly bears, primates and various other critters.

The Harveys are passionate about animals and are dedicated to providing a healthy, comfortable environment for them. Babies are often born at the park, an indication that the animals are happy and well adjusted. Many of the animals are rescue efforts, and this facility was the animals' only chance of survival. The park also strives to educate visitors about the importance of saving endangered species and the urgency to protect their habitats.

As with all privately operated zoos, Safari Zoological Park is exempt from government funding and depends entirely on money raised through admissions, donations and sponsorships. The cost of running such a facility is enormous—large tigers need to eat an average of 15 pounds of meat per day. Funds are also needed to build and improve the animal habitats, as well as to cover veterinary costs.

The economic climate had been tough for the last couple of years, and by July 2008, the Harveys faced a perilous situation. With gasoline prices soaring and operating costs rising, the grim reality was that they needed a miracle by August 1, 2008, to stay open. It was hard to believe they might be forced to close just months before their 20th anniversary.

No zoo operator wants to be faced with these concerns: What will happen to our animals? Where will they go? Who will look after them? The animals, each with their own unique personality and eccentricities, won their keepers' hearts and became part of the family.

It was July 27, and though the Harveys had not resolved their dilemma about the future of the park, a situation at hand was about to upstage the crisis. Sassy, a 10-year-old white Bengal tiger, had gone into labor. She delivered three healthy female cubs, which were named Nasira, Anjika and Siddhani in honor of their native homeland, India.

Sassy and the cubs were doing well, and she fed them that night. The next morning she was beginning to neglect them, and by noon, one of the park guides found the cubs scattered around the habitat instead of tightly nestled next to their mom. A baby tiger needs to eat a lot, and frequently, to survive. Unfortunately, the tigress was rejecting the cubs and had lost interest in nurturing them. Simply put, she was not a good mother. A decision had to be made, and quickly.

Tom was an active member of the Feline Conservation Federation board. He had just returned from a conference in which wildcat specialist Dr. Jim Sanderson announced that there are only about 1300 Bengal Tigers left in India, bringing the total population in the wild to about 4000. Tigers are the fastest disappearing mammals, and statistics indicate that all the wild tigers could be gone in less than 10 years. The world has already lost three species, and two more are on the brink of extinction. Tom was not about to lose these three precious white Bengal cubs.

Allie Harvey had heard on *Animal Planet* about a zoo in Australia that used golden retrievers to nurture abandoned babies. As luck would have it, Allie's one-year-old golden retriever, Isabella, had just finished weaning her own puppies and was still lactating. The Harveys decided to bring the cubs home to see if Isabella's motherly instincts would kick in. It was a "do or die" situation for the tiger cubs.

What happened next not only saved the lives of the tiger cubs but also rescued Safari Zoological Park. When Isabella was presented with the three hungry cubs, she immediately lay down. The babies latched on and instantly started feeding. The foster mom was extremely attentive, licking and cleaning the cubs as if they were her own. Not only were the tigers receiving essential nourishment, they were being showered with loving attention, interaction that is vital to the development of all babies.

Talk about interspecies bonding! Here lay this golden-haired pooch with three fluffy white-and-black-striped tiger cubs suckling eagerly. When the babies cried, it was part screech and part roar, but mama didn't seem to mind.

Isabella was heralded as the golden girl, and she made the national news. The Harveys had prayed for a miracle by August 1. On that exact day, they appeared on NBC's *The Today Show*. In September, they were interviewed by Oprah and were later honored by being voted one of *Animal Planet's* "Top 10 Stories" for 2008.

Isabella, with her amazing maternal instincts, had become an overnight international sensation. All this attention brought visitors from far and wide to the Safari Zoological Park. Everyone wanted to see Isabella and the white tiger cubs.

Isabella nursed the babies through the initial critical stage. Then they were removed to be bottle-fed for the next six months. These were hungry girls and would weigh approximately 300 pounds when full grown. Isabella continued to nurture and interact with her cats as the months passed. This is one cat and dog story where everyone got along.

Creature Feature

Tigers are the largest living wild cats. They have lived on this planet for two million years. Contrary to popular thought, tigers do not live in Africa but reside in the forests and jungles of Asia. Tigers are largely nocturnal and hunt mostly at night. Their night vision is six times better than that of a human.

A Pig Tale

Here is an adoption tale about a special mama dachshund named Tink and her precious pink "puppy."

Johanna Kerby lives with her family on a farm in West Virginia. They enjoy raising pigs for their children's 4-H projects. Early in February 2008, one of the sows delivered 12 babies. One little piglet was extremely small and was the only one born with his eyes sealed shut—not a good sign. Piglets are normally born with their eyes open. They are active immediately and ready to nurse within a few minutes of delivery.

This was the first time Johanna had ever seen a preemie piglet. The wee piglet was breathing well and making noises but didn't have the sucking reflex necessary to nurse. It's easy to test for the sucking reflex; it can be felt by placing a little finger at the back of the piglet's tongue. Every piglet needs this reflex to survive.

Johanna feared the worst and didn't think the piglet would make it. She and her husband, Greg, placed him under a heat lamp and continued with the remaining deliveries, which took up most of the night. After the final piglet was successfully delivered, Greg tried to get the tiny one with the closed eyes to nurse from his mom, but he was too weak to stand up. Greg held the piglet up and managed to squeeze some of the sow's milk down his throat so he could swallow some of the vital nutrients present in the first milk, also known as colostrum. The colostrum is high in antibodies and is critical to a neonatal piglet's survival.

Johanna's two dachshunds, Tink and Sammi, had given birth to puppies a few days before the piglet was born. Sammi delivered seven puppies, and later in the week, Tink had two pups—one of which was stillborn. It was Sammi's first litter, and Johanna was concerned that seven pups would be too much for her, so she placed a couple of the pups with her other "doxie" (an affectionate nickname for dachshund) to foster.

Tink was excited to have more pups and eagerly accepted them as her own. As Johanna watched the attentive mom fostering the pups, she had the idea to bring the piglet up to the house to see if Tink would nurse him too. The plan was a little far-fetched, but she thought it couldn't hurt.

The result was a match made in heaven. Tink loved the tiny pink piglet at once and immediately began to lick him all over. The newborn pig's suckling reflex kicked in, and the wiener dog happily let him nurse.

Johanna named the piglet Pink, a combination of "pig" and "Tink," her dog. She said, "I think Pink's reflex kicked in when the other puppies were nursing. Tink pushed him back toward the puppies, and he just latched on and started nursing!" Then one of the piglet's eyes unsealed; the other eye opened shortly after.

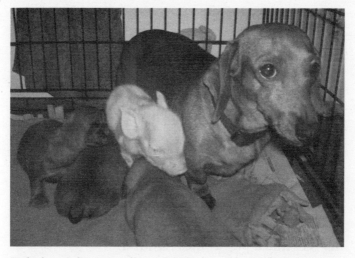

Pink the piglet snuggling with Tink and her "doxie" pups.

Pink made himself right at home with his new adoptive family, curling up with his doxie siblings for long slumbers and regular feedings. Things were looking up for Pink. Johanna and her husband hadn't thought he would live, but live he did!

Pink was just a little larger than the pups and stood out from his brown, furry, big-pawed companions. Here lay this nearly hairless creature, pink as a wad of bubble gum and outfitted with a flat snout and hooves. Pink couldn't have cared less—he was as happy as a clam.

By Valentine's Day, Pink was almost two weeks old and growing healthier and stronger by the day under Tink's mindful care. Almost as though she sensed that Pink had had a tentative start to life, Tink became protective of her piglet and nestled him under her chin to keep him close. Although she licked all her babies, Tink was especially generous with Pink; he was one clean little piggie.

By the time he was six weeks old, Pink was weaned along with the pups. He was now drinking formula out of a bowl and had a healthy appetite, indeed. When the puppies and Pink were together for playtime, Pink sometimes made the mistake of trying to suckle milk from them. Hmmm, the saying "eat like a pig" comes to mind!

His favorite activity, apart from roaming about the house exploring every inch with his little pink snout, was playing with the pups. Pink loved it when they chased him around and then crawled all over him. It was pure entertainment for Johanna and her family to watch.

Almost nine months later, weighing in at 150 pounds, Pink was a healthy, happy pig, rolling in the mud and hanging out with a litter of piglets for company—none of which would have been possible if not for a little dachshund named Tink with a big maternal heart.

The duo became overnight Internet superstars, and photos showing the development of the tiny piglet appeared regularly on the Daily Dachshund and Dog News website. Tink and Pink were even featured on ABC TV's *Good Morning America*. This unlikely pair garnered so much attention and warmed so many hearts that Johanna Kerby wrote a children's story entitled *The Pink Puppy*. It's a story about a mother's love and about adoption. Tink was an excellent role model for the book.

As Andy Warhol said, "Everyone will be world-famous for 15 minutes." Well, Tink got her 15 minutes of fame and then some. But that did not dissuade Tink from once again grabbing the spotlight. Almost one year later, Tink's extraordinary inter-species mothering skills were back at work, and this time her ward was a baby pygmy goat.

The mother goat had died soon after giving birth to triplets, leaving behind one healthy nanny goat, one stillborn and one almost frozen baby billygoat. Greg carried the baby back to the house to warm him up and to try to get some milk into him. Tink was very excited at the prospect of a new baby coming her way and jumped at the chance to care for him.

She lay down on her bed with the little goat, named Spencer, to help warm him. She licked him and followed him everywhere for a couple of days, showering the goat with motherly love and keeping him under her watchful eye. What a sight! Here lay a dachshund, described by writer H.L. Mencken, as "a half-a-dog high and a dog-and-a-half long," nurturing this spindly legged goat covered with jet black hair, except for a fluffy white patch on top of his head.

A family that had other bottle-fed goats soon took in Spencer and his sister, but for those couple of days, Tink enjoyed her role as mommy once again. What a year—puppies, a premature piglet and a baby pygmy goat. I'd say Tink earned the Mother of the Year award.

Johanna wrote to me in March 2009: "Pink is now one year old and doing great! We recently had a birthday party for him and gave him a marshmallow and gummy worm cake. He loved it!"

Mama Mia

The digital age has changed how we communicate. With a few keystrokes, text, image and audio files can be rocketed through cyberspace from one email inbox to another in a split second. Animal lovers like me receive scores of cute critter stories and adorable photographs from friends. Usually they put a big, silly grin on my face, and then I forward them to other animal admirers.

The stories and photos arrive innocently, but to quote Marin Luther King, Jr., "Seeing is not always believing." While the Internet can instantly communicate knowledge and truth, it can also instantly communicate lies.

Oodles of stories are fast-forwarded around the globe, stories that end up being urban legends, folklore, myths, rumors and misinformation. Many of those adorable emails about animals are fiction. Sometimes they are partially true—the photos are real but the accompanying text is not. A little research usually reveals if the story is authentic or not.

One popular story that circulated the Internet describes a situation that occurred in a California zoo in which a mother tiger fell into depression after her premature cubs died. Veterinarians supposedly offered the mourning mother five orphaned piglets, hoping that if she could act as a surrogate mother, her health would improve. A stunning photo shows a sleeping Bengal tigress with five wee piglets wrapped in tiger skin contently snoozing on her body. The image is extraordinary and leaves you in awe; one would expect that a bacon-flavored mid-day snack would be on the tiger's mind, not a nap.

The caption reads, "Take a look...you won't believe your eyes!!!!" Well, in this case the snapshots are genuine, but they do not tell the real story. The photos were taken in 2004 at the Sriracha Tiger Zoo, in Chonburi, Thailand, 50 miles east of Bangkok, not a zoo in California. Furthermore, the tale of the depressed tigress being offered piglets as a substitute for her deceased cubs is pure fabrication.

The Sriracha Tiger Zoo runs a successful breeding program for tigers, with some 400 exotic cats living on the premises. The breeding program does not draw big crowds on its own, so the zoo has created "circus-like" entertainment and exhibits to entice people to visit. The intermingling of species, such as tigers and piglets, was not done to save the creatures' lives but rather as part of a tourist campaign to boost the number of visitors.

The *Pattaya Mail*, an English newspaper serving the east coast of Thailand writes, "The Sriracha Tiger Zoo has a reputation for accomplishing the impossible and creating successful relationships with animals of different species." It appears that by teaching domestic animals such as pigs and dogs, and wild animals such as tigers, to live together peacefully from an early age, these animals are able to continue to cohabit agreeably, demonstrating that unique interspecies relationships and bonds are possible.

Visitors are reported to be both amazed and delighted; perhaps housing tigers, pigs and dogs together in the same enclosure sends a message that we two-legged animals should also be able to live in harmony. So even though the story of the mourning tigress in the California zoo is false, the photos are indeed real—even if the reason for the pairing of the animals is not altogether altruistic. Exercising due diligence is wise when receiving emails that tout, "You won't believe your eyes!"

I have another "unbelievable" animal story to share with you. Once again, what you see is not the truth, but you'll have to wait until Chapter 12!

CHAPTER EIGHT

Best Friends Forever

Animals are such agreeable friends—they ask no questions, they pass no criticisms.

—George Eliot

BEST FRIENDS COME IN ALL shapes and sizes. And, apparently, this is true not only for the human animal, but for many creatures in the animal kingdom as well. The diagram of the food web they used to teach us in school—the one depicting "who eats whom"—is not exactly correct. Incredible stories pop up every day, illustrating that relationships between different and unlikely species are alive and well, and that these alliances offer great benefits to the partners.

Accounts of these interspecies behaviors and bonds also prove that animals are not simply instinctive creatures, relying on innate behavior hard-wired into their genetic make-up. They are, in fact, adaptable beings with a set of needs and complex emotions. They share many of the same basic needs as humans, including companionship.

Interspecies bonds usually involve social animals, so dogs are often front and center in these types of relationships. Centuries of domestication by humans have made dogs extremely sociable and accepting. They have bonded with cats, typically their archenemies, and even voracious predators, such as lions. Interspecies bonds have been documented between household pets, farm animals, zoo inhabitants and creatures in the wild.

When I was 17 years old, we had a squirrel monkey. My family didn't actually go out and seek a monkey as a family pet—it was a gift from my then boyfriend. Imagine my mother's delight!

Our monkey, Kola, just adored our two small dogs. He taunted and teased them endlessly. The party was always on. Kola would race up the stairs with Brandy and Nino in fast pursuit, hit the top stair, springboard to the banister and slide down before the dogs reached the top. The pooches would spin around and bolt back down the steps, and the entire skit would play out again and again. Kola always won that one, as the two dogs finally collapsed to catch their breath.

When Kola was in a particularly cheeky mood, he would jump onto a dog's back, grab hold of its poodle mustache and hang on for a bucking bronco ride. The dog would kick and twist to throw off its rider, but when the game was over, the dog always went back for more. Kola and the dogs enjoyed hanging out together despite their physical differences.

Whatever circumstances bring unlikely critters together, the road to friendship is what counts. And once they become pals, each of their lives is richer because they offer each other companionship, comfort and stimulation—everything you could hope to get from a friend.

Tortoise-loving Hippo

In the wake of tragedy, a small kernel of good news can travel a long way. Such was the case when a photograph of a baby hippopotamus named Owen and a giant tortoise by the name of Mzee appeared in newspapers across the world just days after a tsunami devastated 11 countries bordering the Indian Ocean. The tender picture of an orphaned hippo snuggled up to an enormous tortoise spoke of many things—resilience, determination, kindness and...friendship. It was a story of hope and possibility, something the world needed desperately at that moment.

Owen had been living with his mother in a herd, or pod, in the Sabaki River, one of Kenya's largest waterways. The river flooded because of extremely heavy December rains and washed the hippos downriver toward the Indian Ocean. The pod was now living in salt water near Malindi, a small coastal town north of Mombasa. It was December 25, 2004, and the villagers had tried earnestly for two days to encourage the pod to quit grazing in their gardens and go back upriver, to find fresh water. The hippos wouldn't budge, and when a three-ton animal doesn't feel like moving, there's not a whole lot you can do about it.

On December 26, the tsunami hit. The water rose and fell erratically, and a baby hippo was separated from its mother and the rest of the herd. The baby was stranded on a coral reef among the sea grass. Thousands of people gathered to watch as a small team attempted to capture the 600-pound, two-foot-high infant. Three hours later, shouts of joy could be heard all the way to the next village as the little hippo was rescued. The hippo was named Owen in honor of one of the brave volunteers, who had held him down while a net secured him.

A group of animal caretakers from Haller Park, the largest animal sanctuary in Mombasa, was contacted. Owen needed a home. He was still a baby and had not yet learned how to defend himself or live on his own. The park staff drove for several hours so they could personally pick up the baby. They brought with them a wildlife veterinarian who examined Owen before the long drive back to the hippo's new residence.

An enclosure had been prepared and was filled with plenty of freshly cut grass and bottles of milk. Owen trotted into his enclosure but was not the least bit interested in exploring his new abode. Instead, he beelined for a giant tortoise named Mzee, who was sitting quietly, minding his own business. Mzee was the oldest creature in the park, a whopping 130 years old, and his name fit: *mzee* is Swahili for "wise old man."

Mzee was not initially thrilled with his new roommate; after all, he'd been enjoying his solitude for over a century. The tortoise expressed his displeasure by hissing and crawling away with as much speed as he could muster. Owen was not discouraged and followed the tortoise everywhere he went. The hippo was so young and needed a companion. Mzee was a little bigger but was basically the same shape and color. That fact that Mzee was a tortoise was irrelevant. Owen wanted to be near him, even crouching behind Mzee, just as young hippos hide behind their mothers to feel secure.

It wasn't long before Mzee stopped crawling away, and sometimes, Mzee was the one following Owen. Owen started sleeping right next to the tortoise. Stephen Tuei wrote on the Caretaker Blog on the Owen and Mzee website, "some part of his body always touches Mzee, just like a human child reaching out for some security." Owen would rest his head on Mzee's scaly arm or lay his nose on top of Mzee's shell in pure contentment.

As the days passed, their bond strengthened, and soon they were inseparable. Owen followed Mzee to the pond for a swim, drank when he drank and followed him back out again to eat. It almost seemed that the hippo was copying the tortoise.

Their physical affection continued to grow. They rubbed their noses together, Owen's gigantic, fleshy snout pressed up against Mzee's hard, sharp beak. Owen would nuzzle Mzee's long, wrinkled neck, and Mzee would extend his neck forward looking for more attention. He licked Mzee's face, which the tortoise appeared to thoroughly enjoy. Mzee even put his head in Owen's mouth during a yawn. Talk about trust! It all seemed to be part of their game, an expression of their fondness for each other. Reptiles are not known for their nurturing traits, so this behavior was unexpected.

The two developed a magical way of communicating with each other, their own language, which seemed to evolve from their unique connection. Photographers and videographers documented the following interaction: when Mzee wanted Owen to walk with him, he would walk up to Owen's tail and give it a little nibble, and when Owen wanted Mzee to move, he would nudge his feet or, if necessary, return the nibble. They were gentle with each other and neither was ever injured.

This unusual bond between a mammal and a reptile had never been seen before. No one knew quite what to make of it. Hippos are social animals; tortoises are not. One thing was certain—whatever the reason for this pairing, Mzee helped Owen recover from the ordeal he had suffered, the loss of his mother and family. Mzee offered the friendly hand we all need once in a while.

Newspaper and television crews arrived from around the globe to document this heartwarming tale of friendship and share it with the world, a world still reeling in shock at the horrific losses caused by the tsunami. The story was proof that hope and courage can be found in unexpected places, and that sometimes when you think you are all alone, a good friend just may be nearby, ready to lend a hand.

Creature Feature

The hippopotamus is the third-largest land animal—after the elephant and the white rhino—weighing more than 7000 pounds. It is a plant eater but is considered one of Africa's most dangerous animals. Its huge mouth can open 4 feet wide and consists of lips that are 2 feet wide and canines that grow up to 20 inches long. It can cut a 10-foot crocodile or a canoe in half with one bite.

Bear Hugs

Nature is full of surprises. Its forces are dynamic, revealing wonders and secrets when you least expect them. Norbert Rosing, a German photographer, and Brian Ladoon, a dog breeder, just happened to be in the right place at the right moment to witness a rare and improbable occurrence, one that would catch the interest of scientists and nature lovers around the world.

It was November 1988, on the sub-arctic Canadian tundra. Hundreds of snowy white polar bears were lingering near the unfrozen shores of Hudson Bay, just east of tiny Churchill, Manitoba, the self-proclaimed "Polar Bear Capital of the World." The bears were patiently waiting for the bay to freeze over so they could begin their annual migration north to hunt and feast on seals, their staple food.

Nearby, a pack of sled dogs belonging to Brian Ladoon was tethered on chains, comfortably lounging in a fresh bed of snow as the sun was setting. Norbert Rosing was setting up his camera equipment to capture this tranquil scene when a 1200-pound male polar bear came lumbering out of left field. He was walking slowly and deliberately toward Hudson, Ladoon's prized Canadian Eskimo dog. Panic hit both men. This bear had been fasting for the last four months, and Hudson must surely look like an appetizing meal.

Brian recounted, "At first, I was not sure what was happening. You are always nervous when bears are around. You're watching all the time and learning—you know there is risk."

Bears and dogs are natural enemies, and polar bears have been known to kill and eat sled dogs. The bear closed in so that the two carnivores were face to face. Then something unexpected happened. Hudson remained calm and began to wag his tail as he crouched into a "play" bow. His mouth was open but he was not displaying his fangs and his hair lay flat—all signs that the dog did not feel threatened.

The polar bear was also at ease and responded enthusiastically with non-aggressive body language—soft eyes and flat ears. The message they were sending each other was loud and clear: "Let's play!"

They gently touched noses then engaged in a 20-minute romp. The bear lay down and extended a paw, inviting the dog to play with him. Hudson at one point offered his throat to the jaws of the bear, an amazing act of trust. The two wrestled and roughhoused like old friends.

The polar bear dwarfed the much smaller, 80-pound dog, but this asymmetry of power was not abused. At one point, the bear completely wrapped himself around the dog, giving new meaning to the word "bear hug," and licked the dog's neck. The games continued until both parties needed a break and lay down beside each other, panting happily from their frolic in the snow.

The unlikely playmates were quite simply having fun. Their play signals crossed the species lines, and the polar bear's predatory urges were replaced with a desire to interact and connect. Every evening for almost two weeks, the polar bear returned to play with his canine friend. They danced, embraced and rolled about with abandon. Finally, the ice formed and the bear wandered north in search of food.

No one will ever know for sure why this wild polar bear did not eat the dog. Brian has since seen this interaction between the polar bears and his dogs many times. He says, "It is a good balance... co-existing together for a time."

Rosing's photographs of this rare encounter, witnessed 20 years ago, recently hit the Internet. Millions of people have admired his images, an intimate peek of the unique friendship between a dog and a polar bear.

Something To Crow About

As a kid, the idea of Noah's ark fascinated me. The possibility of all those animals living together, without killing each other, was perplexing. Tigers, goats, crocodiles, pigs and snakes, all happily jammed onto one boat; it boggled my mind.

Nowadays, it seems many unimaginable scenarios are documented in the wild, and often there is no scientific reasoning or explanation. It's just the way it is. Perhaps serendipity is what the world needs more of. Certainly, for one orphaned kitten, a chance meeting with a crow made the difference between life and death.

In August 1999, Wallace and Ann Collito first noticed the tiny stray kitten in their yard in North Attleboro, Massachusetts. They were always fond of animals and in 51 years of marriage had never been without a cat. This one was extremely pretty, with white patches around its neck, hind legs and paws, but it looked too young to be on its own, and the couple was concerned.

A few days later, the kitten showed up again, but this time with unlikely company—a big, black crow. The Collitos couldn't believe their eyes. Here was a crow and a kitten, side by side, running down the road. At first they thought the crow was chasing the kitten. After all, crows eat just about anything, from bugs and worms to furry mice and carrion. Cats and birds are natural foes, but usually it's the cat chasing the bird.

Ann decided to put a dish of food out in the yard, worried that the cat looked thin and was going to starve to death, but apparently, Miss Kitty already had someone providing for her. Wallace shared with *Miracle Pets* during an interview, "The cat was lying down and the crow was picking stuff up out of the grass to feed [her]. He looked like he had a worm or something and he was feeding the cat." The crow foraged for food, snatching a worm or bug, and then held its beak to the kitten's mouth for her to take the item. The Collitos even observed the crow leading the kitten to water. If the kitten was on the road, the crow would start squawking and push her off the road and out of harm's way.

The Collitos named the kitten Cassie and the crow Moses. Their days began to revolve around the activities of this duo, who interacted with each other all day long. The crow would sit beside the kitten and preen its fur. Cassie would lift a paw to clean herself and Moses would grab it playfully with its sharp beak to taunt her. Sometimes Cassie would lie on her back and swat the crow with her paws or pounce on Moses, and a small wrestling match would ensue, feathers and fur tangled together as the creatures rolled around in a ball on the grass.

The crow would retaliate by jumping and flapping his wings at the kitten. The teasing and tormenting would go on for hours, one animal meowing and the other cawing with blissful contentment. Their frolicking was entertaining to watch.

This interaction between the kitten and the crow became their daily routine. The big, black crow acted like the kitten's mother, feeding her, protecting her and playing with her. The Collitos were dumbfounded at this bizarre behavior, so one day Ann called her veterinarian to get some feedback. The vet had never heard of such a thing and advised Ann and Wallace to document the interactions. For the next eight months, they filmed hours of video footage and snapped photos of this implausible relationship.

There was no doubt in their minds that the crow had kept the cat alive. He seemed to know that the kitten needed help. The crow family is advanced in avian evolution. Crows display a highly developed intelligence and a complex social structure. And they are nurturing parents.

One day Ann decided to give the kitten cat food instead of her regular diet of worms and insects. It had initially been difficult to approach Cassie because the crow was protective of its young ward, screeching loudly, swooping and attacking. But this time, the two happily shared the dish of food.

The months passed and Cassie came to trust Ann and Wallace, spending nights inside the house. Like clockwork, every morning at 6:00 AM, Moses pecked on the screen and cawed, a signal that he was outside the door and would like his pal to join him. Moses trusted Ann, and looking directly into her eyes, beckoned her to open the door. Cassie went outside, and the two walked down the stairs together for another day of adventure and play—two best friends off for a day of fun. Cassie returned in the evenings to sleep in the house.

This routine continued for five years, until one day, Moses did not show up. Crows in the wild only live about seven years, so it is likely he died after living an extraordinary life. No doubt Moses' biggest frustration in all those years was the fact that Cassie the cat never got off the ground.

The Odd Couple

The Elephant Sanctuary in Hohenwald, Tennessee, is a special facility developed to meet the needs of elephants, specifically old, sick or needy elephants that have been retired from zoos and circuses. A natural habitat complete with lush vegetation, trees and swimming holes spans more than 2700 acres and offers these elephants the opportunity to enjoy the rest of their lives in a pro-tected home, where they can roam and interact with other elephants.

Just like girlfriends, female elephants like to find a friend that they feel a kinship with—a pal to chum around with. You would think picking a gal-pal would be fairly straightforward when you reside with 17 other trunked "sisters," but a 34-year-old, 8700-pound Asian elephant by the name of Tarra decided her best friend was going to be a dog, and the feeling was definitely mutual.

The chow-mix, named Bella, was found on the property in 2002, "guarding" some large construc-tion equipment that workers had been using to develop newly purchased property. (Perhaps this was a glimpse of insight to her apparent fondness for large objects: Tarra stood over 8 feet tall.) There were 20 other stray dogs and 18 cats that freely roamed the property, but most chose to keep a safe distance from the elephants, and as a rule, pachy-derms are not too interested in barking dogs.

Tarra and Bella felt otherwise and bonded with each other right away. Bella showed a keen interest in the elephant and Tarra reciprocated by petting the dog with her trunk, a gesture that sealed the deal. It wasn't long before the staff noticed the two oddly matched creatures spending all their time together. The pair became inseparable. They ate together and drank together. During the day, they walked about exploring the grounds. At night, they bedded down side by side, with Tarra's foot nudged up against Bella.

Tarra was an active elephant and enjoyed Bella's energetic pace during their daily strolls. The dog showed no fear or intimidation of their 8655 pound weight difference and happily trotted under Tarra's belly, weaving in and out of her legs as they walked. Bella would even roll onto her back, allowing Tarra to stroke her belly with her massive foot.

Carol Buckley, the sanctuary's co-founder, told the *St. Louis Post-Dispatch*, "Elephants are social and so are dogs. Who are we to decide who should be best friends?" Certainly the intense bond that developed between the pachyderm and the pooch was a mutually unconditional and respectful attachment. Tarra and Bella were close, but no one at the sanctuary knew just how strong the bond was until it was tested by a mishap.

Bella and Tarra had been friends for about five years when, one day in April 2007, Bella was discovered motionless in a shallow ravine in the elephant habitat; she could not move her legs or even wag her tail. Tarra had become somewhat protective of Bella, not unlike mother elephants guarding their calves, but on this particular day, Tarra did not object when a staff member gently lifted the dog so she could be rushed to the veterinary hospital.

The x-rays revealed a spinal injury, possibly from an awkward landing or twist while she was jumping over a fallen tree or running through the fields. There was no deep tissue damage or puncture wounds, which was good news. Bella was expected to make a full recovery after an extended period of rest.

The dog was cared for in the sanctuary office, which was separated from the elephant habitat by a wire fence. Every day, Tarra stood faithfully against the fence in quiet solitude, standing vigil for her best friend. With acres and acres of land at her disposal, all she wanted to do was stand in the corner facing the building where her canine pal lay. She seemed to know her friend was unwell and, as friends do, stood by her side.

When Bella was feeling better, Scott Blais carried her to the balcony so the two friends could see each other. Bella's tail immediately began to wag. Scott knew what he had to do next. He told *CBS News*, "We had no choice but to bring Bella down to see Tarra."

Scott carried the pooch down to see Tarra face to face. As Scott approached the fence, Tarra extended her long trunk, reaching to make contact with Bella. She gently probed the dog, touching and smelling. An elephant's trunk contains about 100,000 different muscles and is packed with nerves, especially in the tip. This proboscis is used for breathing, smelling, drinking, grabbing things and communicating. Tarra was reassuring Bella, as well as herself.

Each day, Tarra waited anxiously for a staff member to bring Bella down for a visit. This routine continued daily until Bella regained her strength and mobility. It took three weeks for Bella to recuperate; Tarra's devotion never wavered. When Bella was finally able to wander freely with her companion again, Tarra rejoiced with a round of trumpeting as they strolled off to enjoy the day together.

This remarkable nonhuman relationship displayed all the essential elements of a great friendship: trust, compassion and loyalty. These two overlooked their sizeable differences and celebrated their uniqueness.

~❀~

Creature Feature

Elephants are extremely intelligent, social animals. They live in family groups, working together to rear their young, support the sick and grieve their dead. Elephants communicate with each other through low frequency vibrations. These vibrations, too low to be heard by human ears, can be heard by another elephant up to six miles away.

CHAPTER NINE

Soulmates

A mile or thousands of miles
May separate with distance
Longer than is the Nile
But no matter how far your soulmate is,
You are close and together in the heart;
In tune and close are the spirits,
"'Til death do us part."
A soulmate that is.

—excerpt from "Soulmates" by Agnes Noga

I GREW UP IN A FAMILY that adored animals. We doted on our pets, visited the local zoo and were glued to the television for every episode of Walt Disney and Jacques Cousteau. Animals were regarded with deep reverence, and we were taught to treat them kindly and to be mindful of their needs at all times.

My grandmother would share these fantastic animal stories about life on the farm. She and her nine siblings grew up with the usual barnyard creatures, but there was always a collection of orphaned or abandoned babies and strays in need.

Her mother's philosophy was to help those that needed help, two-legged and four-legged alike. Life was life, and every creature was worthy of care.

My grandmother grew up playing with wolf cubs and skunk babies. Her colorful accounts of these exotic animals set my imagination on fire, and I have to say, our family dogs and birds seemed a little mundane by comparison.

My great grandmother's ease in sharing her home and life with nature's creatures was passed on through the generations, and every member of that clan today lives an animal-rich life. My bloodline is truly critter crazy! So when my mom told me that her cousin Milburn once had a pet bear named Micky, I had to call Milburn to hear the story.

In the fall of 1936, Milburn's father, Albert, was out hunting with a group of men, west of Wetaskwin in Alberta, Canada. They unexpectedly came across an orphaned black bear cub; the mother was dead, and the cub was just a few months old, far too young to survive on its own. Albert scooped the cub up in his arms and took him home.

Albert and his wife, Minnie, lived on a farm with their 12 children, a dog, a cat and an assortment of cows, pigs and chickens. The addition of a bear cub was not that big a deal. Minnie was fairly casual about the whole thing because she was used to unexpected wildlife showing up on the farm. They had raised two orphaned coyote pups a few years back, and the coyotes, now full grown adults, were regarded as valued family members.

This little, black fur-ball was welcomed with open arms. Milburn was 10 years old at the time, and he took a natural liking to the bear. He helped bottle-feed the cub a mixture of milk and eggs, led him out to do his "business" in a box on the enclosed veranda and played with him every chance he could. Micky had a cozy bed of thick blankets, and he slept indoors through the winter.

It wasn't long before Milburn and Micky were best friends. He described Micky as "very playful, clean and intelligent." They wrestled and tumbled on the living room floor, rolling around with big, goofy smiles. "Sometimes when you were lying on the floor, Micky would use his claws to comb through your hair," Milburn remembers. "Even my parents enjoyed him."

Micky always seemed to know when Milburn was coming home from school and would pace restlessly back and forth. Milburn would race up to greet Micky and exchange bear hugs before going off to prepare two or three bowls of puffed wheat and milk. Micky was also fond of Minnie's hot-cakes with homemade strawberry preserves and syrup, and he could gobble down quite a few.

Once spring arrived, Milburn and his brothers dug a good-sized cave in the ground. The den was cool in summer and protected the bear in winter. If the family was ever looking for Milburn, chances were good that he was curled up with Micky, having a nap in the den. Milburn said, "I had no fear of him. I felt special when I was with Micky. I felt proud that he wanted to spend time with me."

Milburn and his pet bear, Micky, playing around

When I hung up the phone after talking with Milburn, I was struck by how vivid and clear his memory was about something that had happened 72 years ago. He talked about his time with Micky as though it was yesterday. It was clear that this animal had deeply touched Milburn when he was a young boy, and he carried those indelible memories close to his heart. Micky the bear had been Milburn's childhood soulmate.

When the Buffalo Roam...at Home

We've all heard the saying, "bigger is better," and when it comes to owning a pet, that's the motto Jim and Linda Sautner, of Spruce Grove, Alberta, have adopted. There's nothing like the love of a shaggy, brown-eyed buffalo to fill your life and your home.

Their tale began when Bailey, the buffalo, was just a baby. His mother abandoned him, so Jim and Linda stepped in immediately and started to bottle-feed the little calf. They were experienced bison ranchers and had intervened on other occasions when a baby in the herd was abandoned because its mother died or the baby was neglected.

Bison *(Bison bison)*, or buffalo as they are commonly called, may appear peaceful and slow moving, but their natural temperament is unpredictable and wilder than that of cattle; usually at around six months of age, their aggressive instincts start to show. As the calves develop, they become playful, romping and kicking around the pasture with energetic spunk. Their massive skulls act as battering rams for butting heads, a popular pastime among young buffalo.

All this buffalo folly is fine if you're a bison, but it is not so attractive if you are a breakable human. So when its aggressive instincts start to kick in, the Sautners wean the calf and introduce it to the rest of the herd, where it will be accepted and have pals its own size to cavort with.

But Bailey was different. Jim recalls, "I've always enjoyed a challenge and had toyed with the idea of taming a buffalo. Bailey had the right kind of disposition, and I decided it was time to try."

When Bailey tossed his head or tried to butt someone, Jim simply corrected him with a deep, firm "Quit!" Bailey actually listened, unlike the other bison in the herd. He would stop what he was doing, look directly into Jim's eyes and calm down. Jim had been the primary caretaker since Bailey was a baby, and despite their enormous size difference, Bailey seemed to know who was boss.

Training was absolutely essential—you can't have a 1-ton, 6.5-foot-tall buffalo mowing over anything and everything that gets in its way. Plus, bison are fast, clocking in at up to 35 miles per hour, which means they can outrun you and most horses. And apart from Bailey's gargantuan size, there was the matter of his horns. A bison's horns can be dangerous, growing 22 to 26 inches long and measuring 2.5 feet across. Clearly, manners were mandatory.

At six months, Bailey was much different than his buffalo siblings—he genuinely liked the company of people, especially Jim's. The bond between them was growing stronger. Jim was discovering the nuances of Bailey's unique personality and learning how to communicate with him. Their relationship was evolving, and their mutual affection was deepening.

Bailey was also fond of Linda and at ease with the Sautners' friends and family members. Soon he was hanging out with Jim and Linda in their home. He was a well-behaved, nine-month-old bison, and the Sautners decided to treat him like a pet and invite him in for a visit. Of course, Linda wasn't completely sure how Bailey would react to being confined within four walls, not to mention what might become of their furniture and ornaments. I know the phrase, "bull in a china shop," would be floating through my mind.

Linda had nothing to worry about, however, because Bailey casually sauntered in through the front door and peacefully settled down in the living room to enjoy the company and the comforts of indoor living. Watching TV was an instant hit; he would sit still and stare at the television set. He also enjoyed being read to. Sometimes Jim curled up next to his mammoth body, and the two indulged in a little shut-eye. Bailey spent an hour or so in the house before getting bored or needing to visit the "buffa-loo" to relieve himself. He always slept near the house, whereas the other 150 head of bison slept off in the field.

Bailey's popularity was growing, and the laid-back buffalo started making appearances at trade shows. The local newspapers loved writing about his sweet nature and gigantic proportions. Then, the *Edmonton Journal* printed a surreal photograph—Jim and Linda seated on their sofa, dwarfed by Bailey towering above them in the

Bailey Buffalo Sr. relaxing at home with owners, Linda and Jim Sautner

middle of the living room. All parties looked relaxed and at home. The photo was irresistible, and it circled the world.

Bailey Buffalo was a celebrity. He was featured on CNN and BBC, in *People* magazine and the *Ripley's Believe It or Not* book, and he even received an invitation to appear on Jay Leno's *Tonight Show*. Unfortunately, because of the BSE (Bovine Spongiform Encephalopathy, or mad-cow disease) crisis of 2003, Bailey was not permitted to cross the border.

The word spread quickly about this world-famous pet bison, and Bailey was invited to A-list events and functions, making appearances all over the province. He met many distinguished and regal individuals, including Queen Elizabeth II and her husband, Prince Philip, the Duke of Edinburgh, as well as political figures and celebrities. Soon his star-class personality hit the silver screen, where he appeared in five Hollywood and European movies. Jim, as his handler and trainer, was always close at hand. The two were pretty much inseparable.

When the duo weren't attending events together, they chilled out in the house at the end of the day—and even danced together. Jim worked with Bailey on a dance routine that involved shuffling hooves sideways and a four-footed hop through the air. It was a real sight.

Bailey the pet buffalo was so popular that on his fourth birthday, April 27, 2004, hundreds of guests

Bailey Buffalo Sr. catching a little shut eye with best friend Jim

attended his party at the Westin Hotel in Edmonton, Alberta. He was a big part of the Sautners' lives and had definitely touched many others.

Nothing could have prepared the Sautners for the dreadful shock four years later when, on April 4, 2008, a freak accident claimed Bailey's life. One of his back legs became trapped in the metal bars of the feeder in his corral. It was the same feeder Bailey had always used, so the Sautners are not sure what went wrong that day. Linda found Bailey lying on his side, struggling to free himself, but too much pressure had been exerted on his heart and diaphragm from being in that position for so long. He passed away soon after, with his head resting in Linda's lap.

At nearly eight years old, he should have had at least another 20 years to spend with his faithful friends. He was taken from the Sautners' lives far too early. They buried him on their acreage with his favorite yellow blanket.

The Sautners were inconsolable; their loss was enormous. They had a difficult time moving forward. Bailey had become a family member, and they had lost their baby. It was especially hard on Jim. He dearly missed his buffalo buddy. They had spent a lot of time together over the years. As long as Jim was at his side, Bailey would go anywhere and do just about anything. Now, there was a big hole in Jim's heart and his life.

Linda confided, "We both know, well, there will never be another Bailey, but Jim and I wondered if there might be another buffalo out there that needed us." Apparently, that was the case. Just three weeks after Bailey's death, the Sautners received a call from a friend. One of her bison cows had died shortly after giving birth, leaving an infant bull calf without a mom. Would the Sautners help?

Jim and Linda didn't hesitate to agree, and their family grew by one, just like that. Jim was working out of town, so Bailey Jr. hopped in the backseat of the Jim's truck every Monday morning, returning Friday night for a weekend at home. Jim managed the bottle-feeding during the week, assisted by eager coworkers.

In no time, Bailey Jr. bonded with Jim and Linda. He traveled well, allowed himself to be led on a halter and enjoyed the attention he received from others. Linda observed that he was a "very healthy boy" that seemed to be "sensible and calm in nature." Most importantly, Linda shared, "he put a grin back on Jim's face."

At two-and-a-half months, Bailey Jr. was still calm, with an easygoing demeanor. The Sautners decided to introduce him to the public at the world-renowned Calgary Stampede. Bailey Jr. was quietly standing in his pen when a First Nations' elder came by to have her picture taken with the buffalo, as she had done for several years in a row. Linda broke the news of Bailey Sr.'s death, and the elder's eyes quickly filled with tears. She asked to go in with the baby and spent a long time petting him, gently touching her face to his before getting up to go.

She confided in Linda that the new calf had "Bailey's spirit within him." This calf had been born within a month of Bailey's death, the time period needed for the "spirit" to transfer. Linda's face did not hide her skepticism, and the elder's next statement was direct: "Look at him, do you think this is normal for a [buffalo] calf?" Four young children were now in the pen with Bailey Jr., stroking and cuddling a content bison calf.

Bailey Jr. was invited to the Indian Village in Stampede Park on the last day of the Calgary

Bailey Buffalo Jr. is blessed by two elders at the Indian Village in Stampede Park, Calgary, Alberta.

❧❀❧

Stampede for a blessing ceremony—an honor not previously bestowed on a buffalo. During a solemn ceremony, using eagle feathers and sweet grass, two elders, Chief Pious and Maggie, gave Bailey Jr. a Native name that translates to "Buffalo Walker," the buffalo that walks among people.

Months have since passed, and the bison calf's personality and behavior have proven to be a lot like those of Bailey Sr.

Linda says, "He loves the people, sleeps with his head in Jim's lap and enjoys Jim sleeping against him." At almost 11 months old, weighing 748 pounds, Bailey Jr. is a healthy, happy bison. He even enjoys leisurely visits in the Sautners' home, just like Bailey Sr. had, and he will hopefully be housebroken soon.

And so as one door closed, another one opened. Bailey Jr. touches the hearts of all those he walks with, just as Bailey Sr. did, and Jim has a new best friend. This teenage bison has some mighty big hooves to fill.

Creature Feature

Horns are permanent, unbranched and hollow. An outer keratinous (a substance similar to fingernails) sheath surrounds a bony core. Horns are found on bison, sheep, goats and cattle. Antlers, on the other hand, are temporary, are made of solid bone and are often branched. They are shed and regrown each year and are found on deer, elk, moose and caribou.

P.S. I Love You

September 6, 2007 is a date that Dr. Irene Pepperberg will always remember; it was the day she lost Alex, her dear friend and colleague of 30 years. They had laughed together, worked side by side, learned from each other and endured the odd frustration over the years. And nearly every day, they said to each other with genuine affection, "I love you."

Alex was Irene's African grey parrot and had been the focus of her research for three decades. The two were in regular contact and developed a deep friendship. It evolved naturally and deepened as the years went by. Alex was a constant in Irene's life; they interacted and exchanged words almost everyday.

The fact that Alex was a bird did not in any way diminish the grief that Irene experienced when he died. She had lost her long-time companion, and his premature death was a tragic blow.

Irene bought Alex from a pet store in 1977 while working on her doctoral degree at Harvard in Cambridge, Massachusetts. At that time, inconclusive research had convinced scientists that a bird could not learn to communicate with humans, beyond mimicking words and imitating sounds. Birds were not believed to possess any potential for language, consciousness or anything resembling human intelligence.

Dr. Pepperberg's work with Alex began with her teaching him the names of everyday objects. She had no idea that this small action would be the beginning of their long collaboration together, that it would be the foundation of her accomplished career in avian learning—discoveries from which would rock the scientific community forever—or that it would jump-start Alex's path to stardom.

Alex was a bright bird, and his owner was extremely motivated and persistent. Before long,

Alex was able to ask for an object using the correct word. They had good days and bad days, but as Alex grew to trust Dr. Pepperberg, he became more confident, and their relationship flourished. He learned more and more words, and Dr. Pepperberg firmly believed that Alex understood that the words referred to specific things and that he was not simply mimicking her words. The scientific world remained skeptical, and her work did not yet garner universal respect.

She continued working with Alex at Brandeis University and Harvard, and through her innovative methods of teaching, the parrot learned more than a hundred English words and could use them in context; he could identify objects and recognize colors, shapes and materials; and he could count small numbers of items. Alex could also sound out words, and he understood concepts such as bigger and smaller, and more and none.

Her findings were often unexpected and revealed abilities that no one had believed a bird could posses. Dr. Pepperberg's work and Alex's stunning achievements changed the way scientists perceived parrot intelligence. Alex and Irene became famous, and Alex was regarded as the world's most amazing talking bird. They were featured on TV shows and written about in international scientific journals and news stories.

Alex had a playful, cheeky personality with a huge vocabulary to back it up. He smugly corrected other research parrots when they answered a question wrong; he delighted in tormenting other researchers with the wrong answers to their questions, and then calling out an apology and the correct answer just as they turned to leave; and he had a list of one-liners, such as "calm down," that he had picked up eavesdropping on other conversations.

This bird was exceptional in so many ways. Dr. Pepperberg realized that he was able to express frustration and apparent boredom. He even expressed jealousy if she paid attention to other parrots. Alex had a big heart; he missed Irene when she was away and loved to tease and joke with her when they were together.

Dr. Pepperberg was a devoted researcher, and the pair worked together day after day, year after year. They got to know each other well, were comfortable in each other's company and were able to "talk" to each other and express basic feelings and needs, as well as humor. This was a much different connection than a bond with a dog or cat.

Alex was much more than just a research animal. However, it remained essential that Dr. Pepperberg's data be collected without an emotional influence or distraction. For her findings to be accepted by scientific minds, her data must be credible and supported by statistics and fact, not emotion-laced observations.

Keeping an appropriate distance was a challenge, because though Alex was never really a pet, neither was he simply the subject of a science experiment. Dr. Pepperberg and Alex were emotionally connected, and this human-animal bond went far beyond the confines of scientific research.

Dr. Pepperberg's groundbreaking research opened the door to understanding animal intelligence. This African grey parrot, with a brain the size of a shelled walnut, was certainly no birdbrain. Alex proved that birds had cognitive abilities and were capable of a great deal more than just mimicking words.

Through his and Dr. Pepperberg's scientific endeavors and long collaboration, Alex single-handedly changed the notion of what a bird is and what it can do. Dr. Pepperberg writes in her book, *Alex & Me:* "By extrapolation, Alex taught me that we live in a world populated by thinking, conscious creatures."

The last time Dr. Pepperberg saw Alex, they went through their usual goodnight routine. She put Alex into his cage, just as she had done for 30 years, and they exchanged words of their mutual affection.

The next morning Alex was found dead in his cage. An examination revealed the cause of death to be heart failure. Alex's obituary hit mainstream media, from the *New York Times* to *ABC News* and

Good Morning America. Thousands of fans sent consolation emails to The Alex Foundation.

The Associated Press printed Alex's last words to Irene Pepperberg, as she put him put into his cage for the night. She recalls the bird said: "You be good. I love you." She responded, "I love you, too." The bird said, "You'll be in tomorrow," and she responded, "Yes, I'll be in tomorrow."

My Pride and Joy

Have you ever gone into a store looking for one thing and come out with something completely different? Maybe you were looking for a pair of pants but ended up buying shoes instead? It happens to everyone, but what makes this story unique is that these two chaps walked out of a store with a lion cub, a decision that would change their lives forever.

The year was 1969, and London was *the* place to be. The "swinging sixties" and the expressive music, art and fashion made the city a creative and cultural hub. Just like in Austin Powers' movies, almost anything and everything was possible in London. For John Rendall and Anthony "Ace" Bourke, two young Australian transplants, the city was much different than their native land.

Life was different back then and—right or wrong—it was actually possible to stroll into a department store, purchase an exotic pet, then walk out and take it home to raise in your urban neighborhood. Sounds crazy, I know, but that was the '60s. When John and Ace heard that Harrods, London's most famous department store, had an exotic animals section, they were curious and decided to check it out.

It was supposed to be a fun outing: a look-and-see kind of excursion. Then John laid eyes on two beautiful lion cubs in tiny cages, and his heart skipped a beat. It was love at first sight, but he was deeply shocked to see how they were living. He grew up in the bush and knew this was not right. He was so disturbed that he decided to rescue one of the cubs. Ace agreed to help, and for 250 guineas, they purchased a living, breathing lion cub.

The two friends worked at a furniture store on King's Road in Chelsea. They persuaded the shop owners that the lion could comfortably reside on the bottom floor and that it would be great publicity for the shop. No doubt, a lion stretched out on a bench would draw in a customer or two. Apparently back then, the government had no problem with a lion living in central London like a house cat.

So Christian the lion, born at the Ilfracombe Zoo in North Devon and displayed in a tiny cage at Harrods department store, was rescued by two determined young men committed to giving him the best life they could.

The two set out to build Christian a home and provide a lifestyle fit for a king. Christian's living quarters were spacious, safe and comfortable. The entire basement was his den, and it was filled with toys and a mattress. He was religious about using his large litter tray. John told the *Daily Mail*, "He had a beautiful, musky smell that was very distinct. But he was clean."

When John and Ace went out, Christian joined them. He became well known in Chelsea, and it was not unusual to see him riding about in the backseat of the Bentley or walking into a restaurant for a night out. The cat had become a local celebrity.

The vicar of the nearby Chapel allowed Christian to race about the walled-in garden. Every day, John and Ace took him there to run around, play football and burn off his "lion's share" of energy. Christian was a growing boy, and exercise was essential. He even enjoyed a swim in the English Channel.

The cat was growing rapidly and required a lot of food—four meals a day, plus supplements. He was expensive to feed and a great deal of work to care for, but there was no question, Christian was worth the effort and the cost. He was an exceptional lion and a joy to be around. Apart from his remarkable intelligence and good behavior, he was extremely loving and gentle to everyone.

The bond between the three grew stronger by the day. There was no fear, only love, trust and respect. The young men were devoted to his care, and they raised him without restraints or physical force. They simply used their voices to indicate what was appropriate behavior and what was not. "He could tell by the tone of our voice," Rendall explained to *The Today Show*. "We ended up with a wonderful animal. He never bit anybody."

Christian loved to nap and cuddle with his owners, roam their flat, rummage through their drawers and get into the usual feline mischief. Their affection was mutual; Christian was generous with his lion hugs, and he greeted them standing on his hind legs, resting his huge paws on their shoulders.

After a year, the men knew they had to find another home for Christian. He had grown from a manageable 35 pounds to 185 pounds. His temperament remained loving, but he was so big he could easily break a window just by leaning on it.

They say there are no coincidences, and one day the universe unfolded in the most fortuitous way. Two actors from the film *Born Free* stopped into the shop. They had played wildlife conservationist George Adamson and his wife, Joy, in the film. The true story was based on how the couple raised the lioness Elsa and reintroduced her back into the wild. The actors suggested that George Adamson in Kenya might be able to help.

George was interested, and Christian and his young owners flew to Kenya. It was quite a moment watching Christian take his first steps on the hot African soil. George had worked out a plan to help reintroduce this tame cat into the wilds of the Kora Reserve. Christian was introduced to a lion who had worked in the movie and who George had released back into the wild. John and Ace stayed long enough to make sure Christian was settled and safe in his new habitat.

George kept in touch with Christian's owners and reported that the British lion was doing well living in Africa. It was early 1972, just one year since John and Ace had left Christian in Kenya, and the pair wanted to go back to see how their beloved cat was doing. There was no guarantee, but they hoped they would be able to find Christian on the reserve.

The reunion was filmed for a documentary, clips of which have been featured on many television shows, as well as the Internet (receiving millions of hits). The moment was deeply emotional and almost beyond comprehension. A full-grown lion slowly approaches John and Ace, with an air of caution. Then, there is a twinkle in his eye as the lion recognizes his roommates. He picks up speed, literally leaping into their arms. Everyone is crying, while giant paws embrace the men, tugging them in for full-body hugs.

The joy of this reunion, for the men and for Christian, was overwhelming. An adult lion, capable of killing these men with a swat, was hugging and purring like a pussycat. The one-year absence had not changed how he felt about them. Christian had spent a year with a pride of lions in the wild, but his bond with these two men was as strong as ever.

Then another incredible moment unfolded. Two lionesses accompanying Christian, neither of which had met John nor Ace, decided to come over and greet them. Christian was certainly a goodwill ambassador.

In 1974, John and Ace received a note saying that Christian was now defending and providing for his pride, and that there was a litter of cubs. Because they were now feeding themselves, the lions rarely returned to camp. It was good news for Christian but a sad reality for his old roomies. Their pet was no longer the tame pussycat they wrestled with in Chelsea; he was now the king of his domain. He hunted, fought battles and defended his family. This was not the lion they knew.

They decided to travel to Kenya one last time, in the hope of one more reunion to say goodbye. But would Christian recognize them this time? It had been two years since they had last seen him. Also, George Adamson reported that Christian had not visited the camp for three months. George did not have any reason to believe that something had happened to Christian, but it was possible that the lion would never come back.

Once again, the stars aligned in mysterious ways. George greeted the men as they got off the plane near the Kora Reserve camp. Christian had arrived the previous night with his lionesses and his cubs. It was as if he *knew* the two men were coming. George told them that Christian was waiting for them by his favorite rock. George and his wife both believed that lions possess a sixth sense and have uncanny telepathic communication skills.

Christian stared intensely at the two men. John and Ace called out his name, and the huge lion walked slowly toward them. John told the *Daily Mail*, "Then, as if he had become convinced it was us, he ran toward us, threw himself onto us, knocked us over, knocked George over and hugged us like he used to, with his paws on our shoulders."

There was another tearful reunion that continued all night and into the morning. They were like old friends catching up, enjoying each other's presence. When morning arrived, Christian walked back into the bush to join his pride. Christian was never seen again.

Though this was their final farewell, John and Ace will always feel proud and blessed to have been members of Christian's "pride," and to know that his legacy and offspring live on, as do their memories of life with this remarkable lion.

Creature Feature

Most cat species live a solitary existence. Lions are the only true social members of the cat family and live in unique groups called prides. The pride's success is based on team-work and division of labor.

My Best Friend Timbo

We humans invest an enormous amount of time trying to change our animals. We train them, we give them rules to keep them safe and to make them easier to live with, we hope they'll grow out of their rambunctious, mischievous younger years (sooner than later) and yet we want them to be themselves so we can enjoy their innate qualities. We ask a lot of them.

But sometimes, it is the animal that changes us. The shift happens so gently and quietly that we don't even realize we've changed. One day, we just wake up and feel a whole lot different. Life is better than it was and, somehow, the presence of animal life encouraged the transformation and helped us evolve to a better place.

Chris Gallucci had the kind of life that needed some changing. He ran away from home at the young age of 12, and by 16, he was doing his first—but not last—stint in prison. His life was out of control—he lived and played with society's "undesirables." Chris grew up fast; rebellion and aggression were his close companions. This lifestyle seemed to be his destiny, and his path through life looked dark and troubled.

One day in 1975, Chris, just out of jail, was offered a job as a welder on the film set of *Roar*. The movie featured Hollywood star Tippi Hedren (from *The Birds*) and her young daughter Melanie Griffith. Tippi's co-stars were an assorted collection of furred and feathered animals. More than 110 untrained lions, tigers, leopards and cheetahs; almost two-dozen flamingos and ostriches; and two elephants also participated in the film.

The movie was filmed on a ranch approximately 40 miles north of Los Angeles, California, bordering the Mojave Desert. Set designers created an African-looking environment to shoot the movie. It was here that Chris first met Timbo, the gigantic African bull elephant. He was instantly intrigued with the animal.

Male elephants are a special challenge because of their massive size and strength, and Timbo had already been dismissed from two zoos for being a troublemaker. The elephant had been brought to the ranch specifically to be part of the movie. Timbo had a reputation for misbehaving, so Chris and the elephant had something in common.

When the film's elephant trainer quit, Chris applied for the job at once. What he didn't realize was that he was about to learn a few lessons from the largest land animal on the planet. Chris recently reflected about his life back then on his website, "My life before here was craziness, and even if you're afraid, you can't show it." Not showing fear was a good approach to begin working with Timbo.

Chris took a novel approach to win Timbo's trust that first night. He wanted to be accepted by the great pachyderm, so he chained himself beside Timbo in the elephant's enclosure and tossed the key. And so began their 30-year-long journey together, a journey that would turn Chris' life around.

Caring for an elephant is an enormous task and takes up a great deal of time. There is the preparation of food and feeding, cleaning the animal and the enclosure, taking long walks for exercise, initiating training sessions, promoting regular interaction for stimulation and performing routine health checkups. Most zoos have multiple keepers on the elephant shift, but Chris was Timbo's only guardian, 24 hours a day and seven days a week. The film took five years to complete, and the two got to know and understand each other well along the way.

Once filming had wrapped up, Tippi purchased the land of the film set to establish the Shambala Preserve, an 80-acre animal refuge for the animal stars of *Roar*. Chris stayed on to continue caring for Timbo. He had developed a deep relationship with the elephant, one that filled his heart and gave him purpose. When he was with Timbo, he thought like an elephant. These two souls were linked in kinship. Chris made a promise to Timbo that he would stay with him until the day the elephant died.

And so for the next 25 years, Chris honored his promise and dedicated his life to his best friend. He kept a diary about their life together and the connection that developed between them. Excerpts from his diary and a series of photographs capture the depth of this bond in a book entitled, *The Elephant Man*. Chris wrote, "I live with an elephant and an elephant lives with me. We belong together. And we understand each other. I have the nature of an elephant. And he has my character. After 25 years, this is completely normal."

Timbo died of heart failure on June 5, 2005, at the age of 48. The remarkable 30-year relationship, one that had saved Chris and pointed his life in a new direction, came to an abrupt end. The largest and oldest African bull elephant in the United States had tamed this wild man with nothing more than the honesty of his nature.

Chris and Timbo shared a deep spiritual connection, a bond that gave Chris a life to be proud of and a future to look forward to. Chris continues to work at the Shambala Preserve, offering their many endangered exotic cats—castoffs from private owners, zoos and circuses—a safe and comfortable place to live out their lives.

Section Four

Encounters with the Animal Kingdom

Until one has loved an animal,
a part of one's soul remains unawakened.

–Anatole France

Animal enthusiasts can be a bit kooky when it comes to critters. They will travel clear around the world just to take a peek at animals in the wild. These nature lovers spare no expense, subject themselves to discomfort and even put themselves at risk, all so they can be close to the animal kingdom, even for just a moment.

Animal encounters are often a combination of luck, opportunity and timing, and when they occur, it is pure magic. Whether you watch a mama bear amble through a stream with her cubs, clumsy-footed and awkward, in tow; cry out "thar she blows" as a stream of misty air and vapor shoots from the blowhole of a magnificent humpback whale; or tingle at the eerie thrill of having a large, toothy wolf-eel slide across your palm while scuba diving, animal encounters are profound and memorable.

First there is the initial elation when you spot the animal. Then, a wave of stillness takes hold as you marvel at this moment of perfection nature has cast your way. Afterward, there is reflection and perhaps a deeper understanding of what the encounter meant not only to you, but also to the animal.

For me, there is something humbling and reassuring about being in the company of animals. It's like having a privileged peek into a private world. It reminds me of our connectedness with all living things—that we are all in this together. It seems to affirm our humanness while reminding us of our animal roots.

There are many opportunities designed to offer anyone with the desire and curiosity an intimate and personal experience with animals: whale watching, swimming with dolphins or diving with sharks, to name but a few. You can even take a ride on an ostrich! These are mouthwatering adventures if you have a sweet tooth for animals.

And if you don't want to get your hair mussed, tamer excursions such as a guided tour through the national parks or a stroll through the world-famous San Diego Zoo or the Monterey Bay Aquarium can make you feel as though you are a million miles from home.

The only thing that matters is that for a brief moment in time, you are captivated with the beauty and splendor of animal life.

CHAPTER TEN

Animal Magnetism

Wherever different minds meet in the spirit of fellowship, there we find a great harmony, peace, happiness, understanding and cooperation in life's activities.

—Paramabansa Yogananda

THRILL-SEEKERS FLOCK FROM around the world to Churchill, Manitoba, with the hopes of spotting, from the safety of their tundra buggy, one of the most dangerous and efficient hunters on the continent: the polar bear. Talk about an adrenalin rush.

One of my most intimate and unexpected interactions with wildlife occurred while I was photographing a mother zebra and her baby in Zimbabwe. The mother was suckling her foal in a clearing just off the side of the road. I was using a 300 millimeter zoom lens and stood at a respectful distance so as not to disturb or frighten her and the baby. It was a tender moment, and I was sending out my "I love you" energy as I snapped shots.

At one point, the mother looked directly into my eyes and walked slowly and surely toward me. She got so close that one eye, fringed with long lashes, filled the entire frame. The baby continued suckling milk as if I wasn't even there. It is a moment that I will never forget.

For those who spend a lot of time in the great outdoors, working, playing or pursuing a hobby, the likelihood of encountering a wild animal increases. Sometimes these rare moments are pivotal in a person's life; they are mystical meetings that leave one changed forever.

The following stories are tales of trust, mutual respect and kindness, where an unexpected encounter allowed observers to see life through new eyes.

Grizzly Close-Up

Albert Karvonen is an internationally renowned producer and cinematographer of natural history films. He lives in the small town of Boyle, Alberta, surrounded by pristine wilderness, and he has spent much of his life traveling across North America and abroad, trekking from mountaintop to shoreline, documenting the lives of animals in 120 films. Over the decades, he has been touched by many extraordinary experiences, events that have made him passionate about the natural world and adamantly protective of the environment.

He has been filming animals in the wild since 1960 but had never set eyes on the legendary grizzly bear. Through the ages, fascination with the grizzly (also known as the brown bear) has inspired deep and powerful emotions, ranging from fear and contempt to awe and spiritual kinship.

Although some herald the animal as an icon of courage and strength, the grizzly remains much maligned and greatly misunderstood by the public. The grizzly is the second-largest and most powerful land predator, beaten only by the polar bear. A large male can weigh over 1000 pounds and tower almost nine feet on his hind legs. In a word, grizzlies are intimidating.

Albert had heard a lot of stories about grizzlies, many with conflicting views. These secondhand bear stories piqued Albert's interest, and in 1980, he decided to find out about grizzly bears himself and to do a film entitled *Grizzlies of the Great Divide*. Whereas some outdoorsmen are trophy hunters, interested in conquering the grizzly as a symbol of bravery, Albert only wanted to "see them, experience them in their natural habitat and film them," so he could share the wonder of their lives with others.

Albert scouted for a location to establish base camp and found the ideal spot on the Alberta-British Columbia border in the Rocky Mountains. He prepped the area for two months, constructing a crude 10-foot-by-12-foot cabin for sleeping, eating and storing gear. The structure was so well camouflaged with a moss-covered dirt roof and dried logs that the pilot had to make two passes before he could spot the cabin when he dropped off Albert and his gear several weeks later.

The cabin, sparsely furnished with two cots, sleeping bags and a table, was on top of a hill overlooking the valley. It offered a breathtaking panoramic view of the area but more importantly, it was a good vantage point from which Albert could easily spot grizzlies wandering through the area.

Next, he needed numerous blinds spread throughout the area to conceal himself and his camera gear. It was essential not to disturb or frighten the animals so he could film their true behaviors in the wild. Albert assembled well-camouflaged blinds out of logs, cutting a small hole in each for the camera lens. He built these sturdy structures in three different locations: in the meadow, near the river and higher in mountains. They were positioned a safe distance—a little over half a mile—from base camp.

Then he set up a tape recorder with a sophisticated microphone that was sensitive enough to pick up the activities of the bears rustling in the bush, playing together and eating, as well as a variety of natural ambient sounds including wolves, birds, wind and water flowing in the stream.

The first trip to the area that summer was exciting and held a lot of unknowns. He baited the area in front of the blinds with a beaver carcass obtained from a local trapper, hoping it would lure the grizzlies. Before long, a mama bear and her two beautiful babies arrived to feast on the carcass, and Albert, secretly tucked in a blind, started to film his first grizzly bear encounter.

"The mother grizzly was in the meadow with her two cubs behind her. She started to walk slowly toward me. I was in the blind so she couldn't see me, but she knew something wasn't right because she stopped abruptly three or four meters [10 or 13 feet] from the blind and looked me directly in the eye. She held one paw in the air, as dogs often do when they are a bit anxious or wary about a situation. Then the grizzly turned suddenly and walked away with her cubs."

That was Albert's first intimate encounter with a mother grizzly. He would never forget how she stared deeply into his eyes. Through the excitement, he remained quiet, focused on filming, as her head slowly filled the entire frame. Albert was totally engrossed in the moment.

He rolled film at every opportunity that year, keen to observe the bears' behavior and pick up clues that would help him safely document these grand, but potentially dangerous, animals. By the end of the shoot, Albert had recorded some excellent footage of the bears and had acquired firsthand knowledge about their lives and behaviors. He was fascinated with these animals and had become a grizzly bear enthusiast.

He returned the following year and was happy to see that the mother and her cubs were still living in the area. The cubs had grown a lot but remained dependent on their mother. They followed her lead and stayed close; she taught them how to forage for food and other skills they would need to survive on their own. Each day, Albert gathered footage of the sow and her two cubs interacting with each other and the other bears in their surroundings. He was starting to understand life from a bear's point of view and was gaining valuable practical knowledge about how to deal with them in the field.

Albert's wife, Pirkko, joined him for a few days and brought along some whitefish to bait the area. Pirkko waited at base camp while Albert hid in the blind so he could film the three bears as they gobbled up the fish. The mother bear lifted her head and walked toward the blind. Albert continued filming the bear as she approached, her body growing larger with each step.

Finally, Albert removed the camera from the hole and peeked out to see exactly how close to the blind the mama bear was. To his surprise, he was met with another eye. There they were, man and beast, eye to eye. Nobody moved. Finally, she sauntered away, walking in the direction of base camp.

The three bears arrived at camp and, being the curious creatures they are, busied themselves with a thorough investigation. Pirkko could hear the bears sniffing around on the other side of the log wall from where she sat. The bears were loud, huffing

Mama grizzly bear with her two cubs nearby

and grunting as they inspected everything in sight. She was relieved when they finally headed off.

That was Pirkko's last trip to base camp. She told Albert, "If you want to die this way you can, but I am not coming here again." And she didn't.

For Albert though, it was pure adrenalin. His eye-to-eye encounter was a memorable moment, the ultimate interaction to date, and he was not the least bit reluctant to continue. In his mind, his relationship with the bears was just beginning.

Albert went up for his third visit in 1982, this time accompanied by a still photographer. The two cubs, brother and sister, had disengaged from their mom and were now living independently. The pair enjoyed hanging out together, hunting, playing and exploring the area. The cubs had seen Albert now for three years in a row and were starting to accept his presence. A relationship was developing between him and the bears, one that he felt honored to be part of.

The bears' interest in Albert had grown, and one day they decided to visit him at base camp. Bears are bright, inquisitive animals with keen senses; they knew exactly where to find him. The first incident involved the porridge pot. The bears quickly discovered where the porridge pot was cleaned out every morning and came around to lick the morsels on the ground.

Their curiosity was unfolding in the most astonishing way. The cubs were now coming to base camp on a regular basis to investigate and visit. They seemed relaxed and calm around Albert, and he began to film them out in the open. This was a remarkable opportunity, and for a filmmaker it offered a huge advantage—Albert no longer had to be hidden in the blind to observe the bears.

They sniffed about, stood on their hind legs to get a closer look through the base camp window and used their massive paws, armed with razor-sharp claws, to rip, grab and examine whatever caught their fancy. Rubber boots left outside the cabin became toys to play with and chew. A few pairs of socks were left hanging to dry on a nearby tree. Those socks were never worn again.

The clever cubs were interested in everything, making them exciting subjects to watch and film. Albert remembers opening a tin of turkey stew that was so unpalatable, even by roughing-it standards, he just could not eat it. So, he found an area away from the cabin to dump it. Well, the cubs caught wind of the scent and showed up in no time to check it out.

They weren't too keen on the recipe either because instead of eating it, they took turns rolling in it, smearing the stew all over their fur. Bears eat just about anything, so this was a poor review of the stew!

Over the course of almost two weeks, the cubs came around daily, and Albert was able to capture their entertaining antics on film. To Albert, these grizzly cubs seemed like "playful and mischievous balls of fur." They loved to wrestle, tumbling about and chasing each other for the sheer fun of it. Albert loved the hours he spent observing his fluffy subjects.

Each day a brand new scenario unfolded, and Albert felt privileged to be able to witness it. He believed the bears had "befriended" him in a respectful, observant way, and he continued to film them out in the open, both from base camp and the surrounding grassy and treed areas.

Bears communicate with one another using body language and a variety of distinct vocalizations. A huff, woof or growl usually means the bear is agitated, annoyed or angry, while a mumble, hum or purr often indicates contentment.

One day, the cubs wandered into the meadow not far from base camp. Albert along with the photographer set off to film them. Albert wanted to try and get some shots of the bears standing up on their hind legs. He set up the camera and tripod in front of them and started to film as they snooped around and sniffed the ground.

"They don't usually stand up, so I made a little *huff* sound to see what would happen. The male stared directly at me and stood up on his hind feet to get a good look." Albert remained silent and filmed the moment.

Then the bears wandered off into the bush. Albert was a little startled when he heard rustling in the bush behind him. He whipped around to see the two cubs standing there. The bears had circled 180 degrees around to investigate the situation and were now standing behind the men. Both men were fully exposed to the grizzlies. Albert remembers, "The male cub stood up tall and 'huffed' right back at us."

Even though these bears were still cubs, they were at least 220 pounds and were certainly large enough to take down a grown man if they wanted to. Albert remained still and said in a soft, even tone, "All we are trying to do is take some pictures. You are beautiful, good-looking guys."

The bears listened to him speak. He had their attention, and they seemed to feel no threat. Then he said, "OK, you know what I think? I think we are OK," and the pair calmly turned around and sauntered back into the bush.

Albert and the bears were establishing some sort of rapport. He was grateful for what he had learned about bears during the previous two years of filming: do not scare, offend, surprise or threaten them; give them lots of space and respect; and always talk in a soft, low, calm voice. This interaction was a pivotal moment in his life. Albert says, "It reinforced my belief that if you accept bears the way they are in the wilderness, they will accept you."

One day, Albert was in the open, filming the cubs as they went through their routine inspection of base camp. Unexpectedly, the larger male raised his head and focused on Albert, intent on getting a little closer than usual. Albert was filming with a 50–300 millimeter zoom lens, so as the bear advanced, it got bigger and bigger until its huge head filled the frame. The grizzly continued to move forward.

Albert calmly suggested to the bear in a low, soothing voice, "I don't think you should come any closer." The bear stopped in his tracks to listen, then dropped his head to the ground, pawing a rotten log, before nonchalantly wandering away.

By the end of July, Albert was ready to wrap up the shoot and head home. He had gathered some terrific footage and had lots to share about bear behavior and his interactions with them. He was confident that he had gathered enough material to complete his film. Apparently though, the male cub was not convinced and was about to lend a hand, or "paw" as it turned out.

Two cameras were running out in the open near base camp; one was automatic, and Albert was operating the second. Suddenly, the male bear became interested in the lone camera. He walked up to the camera on his hind legs, as a human would, placed his enormous paw on the tripod handle and recorded the scene. Three years of filming and the grizzly bear got the last shot!

Albert fondly recalls his bear encounters as the "ultimate intimate experience with a grizzly." He says, "I knew there was risk, but I never felt seriously threatened." According to Albert, the encounters affirmed the "infinite potential and spirit of the natural world," an ideal that inspired Albert and had motivated him to make natural history films.

His personal experiences with the grizzlies and the remarkable relationship that evolved between them were intensely spiritual and deeply moving. They had a profound effect on his life and motivated him to continue making films for another three decades. Is it any wonder that the final scene in *Grizzlies of the Great Divide* is the one taken by the grizzly bear?

Creature Feature

Female bears have evolved "delayed implantation," whereby the fertilized embryo does not implant into the uterine wall until late fall, just before the mother enters her den. If the mother has enough fat reserves to sustain a pregnancy, the embryo will implant and develop into a cub; if not, the embryo will be reabsorbed into her body.

The Butterfly Effect

As a toddler in Lincolnshire, England, Ian Sheldon was fascinated by butterflies. He found the intricate designs on their brightly colored wings mesmerizing as they flew, weaving an erratic path through the family garden. He was devoted to watching them, and his parents bought him a net when he was three years old. So began his hobby of collecting, identifying and studying the lives of these winged beauties—a passion that spanned more than two decades.

By the age of four, Ian and his family were living in South Africa, where he could admire more than

600 butterfly species, many far more colorful than those in England. He was in butterfly heaven and spent every available moment outdoors focusing on his hobby, expanding his collection and getting to know the habits and peculiarities of the butterflies of the southern hemisphere.

When Ian turned 11, the family moved once again, this time to Singapore. This was good news for a lepidopterist—there were almost 300 species of butterflies in the area, the two largest parading a wingspan of seven inches.

His knowledge of these beautiful insects continued to grow, as did his collection. Like most children, he was captivated by the butterfly's unusual life cycle: the transformation from the caterpillar stage (larva) into the inactive pupa (chrysalis) and the emergence of a colorful winged adult. Metamorphosis is one of the great mysteries of nature and has fascinated humankind since the beginning of civilization.

Ian fondly remembers rearing a brood of tortoiseshell butterflies; he collected several dozen eggs off a stinging nettle plant and hatched them in a mesh cage. He tended to the caterpillars, giving them water and nettle leaves until they entered their dormant pupa phase. When the chrysalis turned transparent, Ian could see the brilliant orange and brown markings on the wings and knew they were close to hatching.

Watching them hatch was thrilling: the cocoon would crack open, and a fully developed butterfly would emerge, hanging upside down to allow the wings to unfurl. When the last one had hatched, Ian took the cage of butterflies outside and sat it in the sun. He opened the door and witnessed their "explosion of freedom into sunshine," a mass of color swirling though the air, returning to land on the cage several times before leaving for good. His innate curiosity of butterflies had led to a wonderful hobby.

Ian's enthusiasm for butterflies continued through his university years in Cambridge, England. Like most collectors, he had a constant craving to expand his collection. He describes it as a "hunger." During his final year at Cambridge, he went off to the jungles of Borneo to study a population of local butterflies. He continued collecting and pinning specimens and published a paper with his findings, earning an honors degree in zoology.

Life until his mid-twenties was largely governed by his passion for butterflies—researching, collecting and pinning. It was a hobby that he devoted a great deal of time to and one that brought him great pleasure. He was also becoming a well-known artist, illustrating dozens of animal and insect field guides for naturalists.

He continued his education at the University of Alberta, studying ecotourism for a masters of science degree. It was immediately obvious that his butterfly-collecting hobby was a problem.

Ecotourism boldly promotes the philosophy "look, enjoy, leave." Touching was a "no-no," and killing anything for the purposes of collecting was an absolute crime.

Ian was faced with a dilemma. Ecotourism's "take only pictures, leave only footprints" approach to enjoying nature was in direct conflict with butterfly collecting, an important part of his life. It was a quandary, and Ian was about to go through a transformation of his own.

Determined to continue with his studies, Ian went to Thailand to gather research for his thesis, only this time his research did not involve collecting and pinning. Instead, he talked with tourists about their perceptions and expectations of tourism. He spent four months in Thailand, strolling through dozens of national parks, interviewing hundreds of tourists.

One day near the town of Chiang Mai, Ian was sitting on a park bench waiting for the next group of tourists to wander by. He spotted one of his most sought-after butterflies, the great egg fly, darting through the air just 30 feet away. It was an excellent flyer with acute eyesight, quick movements and "supersonic" butterfly speed.

The butterfly that had eluded him for years was zigzagging straight for him. Ian reflected on the joy he would have once received by adding this admirable butterfly to his collection. What happened next was surreal: the great egg fly landed on his chest, directly on what Ian described as his "heart center."

Ian bent his head and stared into the creature's great, spherical, compound eyes, and a matrix of hexagonal lenses appeared to stare right back at him. This magnificent insect had a wingspan of almost four inches. It lingered for a long time on his chest. This was unusual because he was not standing in the sun, nor was he wearing a flowered shirt, cues that would normally attract such attention. This event was not so much an accident as it was a gift.

Ian recalls, "It was like the butterfly was saying 'Thank you for the change you have made in your life.'" The butterfly finally lifted and flew away. Ian was truly moved. This extraordinary encounter altered him and marked a transition in his life. He was no longer a butterfly collector, and perhaps this was nature's way of showing her gratitude.

Talking Prairie Dogs

Prairie dogs have been regarded as nuisance animals for a long time. They are perceived as pests that destroy ranch land, causing cattle and horses to break their legs in the tunnels, spreading disease and multiplying so quickly that they suffer from overpopulation, therefore deserving no legal protection.

Contrary to these myths, prairie dogs do not destroy the environment or cattle and are, in fact, crucial to the prairie ecosystem. Old myths die hard, and they are still considered vermin in many places. One July weekend in 1990, the small town of Nucla, Colorado, hosted its first annual "Top Dog World Championship Prairie Dog Shoot," killing 2956 prairie dogs in just two days. How could these cute, furry little critters cause so much hoopla and be the victims of so much hostility?

Today, some species of prairie dog are endangered or threatened, and as a result, the animals that prey on them or depend on them for shelter, such as the black-footed ferret, the burrowing owl and the prairie rattlesnake, are also endangered. The lesson is the same one we learned in school as a child: all living things are interconnected.

A biologist by the name of Dr. Constantine "Con" Slobodchikoff has been studying the communication and social behavior of Arizona's Gunnison's prairie dog for more than 20 years. He has discovered that the animal's vocalizations are actually a highly sophisticated alarm call system that relays information through barks, yips and chirps about a predator that is approaching their colony.

While Con was unraveling the secrets of this complex language, the city of Flagstaff, Arizona, home to a large resident population of prairie dogs, was about to level their prairie dog town to construct two new soccer fields. The community had observed these prairie dogs for years and was in an uproar over this cruel plan. They enjoyed watching the activity in the colony, heads popping out of burrows and the greeting exchange of affectionate kisses, as well as listening to the animals' high-pitched banter. The prairie dogs were an integral part of their community.

The community's unhappiness created so much attention that a plan was designed to relocate the prairie dogs to privately owned property, a vacated colony complete with holes and tunnels. Black-footed ferrets, which rely heavily on prairie dogs as their staple diet, had wiped out the previous inhabitants.

Unfortunately, before the plan could be initiated, bulldozers leveled a portion of the colony's hibernating prairie dogs, burying them—much to the horror of neighboring families. A TV producer with CBC's *Country Canada* heard about the situation in Flagstaff and wanted to do a story about the "importance of saving the prairie dogs" and "why people should care." Cameraman Kent Martens of Edmonton, Alberta, was assigned to film the story.

Kent had gained a lot of experience over the years working in the field filming wildlife. He'd been soaked to the skin while filming eagles in the rain during a salmon run, knocked over while stalking a wild boar in the bush and had hiked camera gear through the frozen snow drifts of the Yukon to track wolves. Prairie dogs were going to be a breeze.

As it turned out, Kent had a little experience in the prairie dog department. As a youngster, he had trapped one in a box and proudly carried it home.

It seemed like a good idea at the time but didn't turn out so well. Kent was bitten by the frightened prairie dog; his Dad was upset because there was a rodent in the kitchen and Kent had to walk all the way back to its burrow to return it. All in all, it was not a great experience.

Kent flew to Flagstaff in the spring of 2000 to spend five days filming the relocation of the prairie dogs and to tape a number of interviews. He thought it was an interesting story but was rather ambivalent toward the little guys. That was about to change.

While recording Con's interview, Kent was taken aback to learn about the highly developed communication system of the prairie dog. Con described how he recorded their language with a microphone and then analyzed it with an advanced software program. Studying the wave patterns, he found that they used an array of words, each with a specific meaning, and showed signs of sentence structure. It was a remarkable discovery.

The prairie dogs' alarm calls actually provided a description of the predator—different calls were issued for different predators. In fact, the animals could communicate the color of a human's clothing and whether they carried a gun or not. Their escape responses varied depending upon the species of predator: they would run to the burrow and dive inside for hawks and humans, and stand upright outside the entrance for coyotes and dogs. This certainly said a lot about the cognitive possibilities of these unassuming animals.

As the interview progressed, Kent's attitude toward the prairie dogs started to change. He saw them not just as animals but also as sentient or conscious beings that could share information with each other.

"My affinity with them...my empathy, grew by leaps and bounds. I realized that they could communicate with each other about their lives. I couldn't talk to them, but I knew that information was being passed between them."

It was an eye-opener—a realization that changed the way he looked at the animals. They were still furry, little, pot-bellied critters *but* there was something else going on, something more intelligent than he had thought possible.

On the day of the relocation, Con supervised dozens of volunteers as they worked with the Arizona Game and Fish Department to trap, crate and load the prairie dogs into trailers. They mapped out the existing colony holes and numbered them to track which animals came from which burrows. Prairie dogs live in a complex social network, and a great effort was made to relocate family groups as a unit.

The animals were frightened, so the volunteers placed a burlap cloth over the crate to help calm them. A convoy of quads hauled the trailer full of prairie dogs up into high country, to their new home. The group gathered in a circle to pray for the prairie dogs before releasing them to their new holes.

Kent filmed the good feeling that resonated from the group. These prairie dog lovers had worked hard to save the lives of the prairie dog town. The experience had a profound effect on Kent and changed the way he felt about other animals, as well.

Kent Martens, ready to introduce the crated prairie dogs to their new colony

"This was not just a curious incident—it literally changed my world. It marked the beginning of a new way of how I look at the animals that are here in the world with me. We may think that animals do not communicate, so it's easy to dismiss them. But once you understand that they are actually talking among themselves, your view of the animal kingdom shifts. It changes our relationship with them and establishes a sort of kinship."

The prairie dog town had sent a message using yips, yaps, barks and chirps that touched this man. Kent learned that the prairie dogs had a lot to say to those that would listen. It was a story he felt honored to film and share with a nation.

Creature Feature

Prairie dogs are social animals and live in closely knit family groups called coteries. These coteries are grouped together into "wards" (or neighborhoods) and several wards make up a "colony" or "town." The town is connected with a series of tunnels containing separate rooms for sleeping, rearing young, storing food and eliminating waste.

In the Company of Wolves

Few careers come close to offering the excitement and challenge of wildlife filmmaking. This profession, driven by a passion to observe and experience the natural world, requires an enormous amount of patience and tenacity, as well as good survival skills for coping with whatever comes your way.

Andrew Manske has been working as a wildlife cinematographer, director and editor for more than 14 years. He has spent incalculable hours in the field, hunkered down in observational blinds by day and tents and lookout towers by night. His quest is to capture the lives of animals in their natural habitat and share their secrets with audiences around the world.

His enthusiasm to promote awareness of our environment and the animal kingdom has been featured in more than 40 natural history films and documentaries, and has brought him face to face with grizzlies and polar bears, bison, mountain goats and birds of prey. He has endured difficult northern environments and harsh weather, always aiming to get the shot, even if it means hanging out of a helicopter.

Andrew has always had an affinity for wolves: their beauty, power and intelligence make them exceptional subjects, but it is the challenge to actually film them that has his attention. "For a filmmaker they are fascinating animals, and not a whole lot has been done on them. They are a secretive species and extremely difficult to find and film. I like a challenge."

Traveling throughout North America, Andrew has filmed the lives and habits of these mysterious animals several times. Each experience furthered his interest in them, especially how their hunting strategies appear to vary in different environments.

In Canada's Northwest Territories, Andrew filmed wood bison in 1995. These massive, one-ton animals roam the Mackenzie Bison Sanctuary, which is an area made up of boreal forest and wetland meadows. As he filmed the shaggy beasts, he noticed that packs of wolves showed up and tried to herd the bison in the hopes of taking one down. The wolves' hunting behavior interested him so much that he returned years later to spend more than a year documenting the relationship between the gray wolf and the wood bison.

He traveled to the Rocky Mountains to film wolves in Jasper, Alberta, and Yellowstone National Park, Wyoming, as they tracked a herd of elk, also known as wapiti. The wolves' hunting strategy for wapiti was different than it was for wood bison; they modified their tactics to suit the prey animal. This was an exciting discovery.

Andrew headed to the northeast coast of Canada to document the elusive wolves of Labrador. It was an ambitious expedition and demanded an intense effort. Andrew filmed for more than two years, subsisting in the field for 150 days.

For two to three weeks each year, one of the largest barren-ground caribou herds in the world—the George River Caribou Herd, with more than 500,000 individuals—funnels through a canyon crossing as they migrate from the calving grounds of the Arctic coast to winter in the lichen-rich boreal forest of Labrador.

As thousands of caribou stream by, packs of hungry wolves lay waiting in ambush. Andrew was rewarded for his rough existence in the wilderness with stunning footage of the wolves in action.

His fondness and appreciation for these animals grew as he unraveled fact from mystery and myth. Contrary to popular belief, most wild wolves are wary of people. On more than one occasion, he had lost the perfect shot because the wolf had picked up his scent and bolted.

He remembers filming a black wolf that had leapt over a creek to take down a lone caribou calf. It was an amazing sequence to capture on film and Andrew, carefully hidden in the blind, was bubbling with excitement. "Just as the wolf was about to take down the caribou, it literally 'put the brakes on' and ran. The wolf had caught my scent." Decades of persecution by trapping, hunting and poisoning have wisely taught the wolf not to trust humans.

Andrew did not carry a gun and had never felt threatened by the wolves. If anything, he felt

234 AMAZING ANIMALS—ENCOUNTERS WITH THE ANIMAL KINGDOM

a deep respect for and kinship with them. He became familiar with the dynamics and social structure of pack life. Wolves are social carnivores, and relationships and bonds are extremely important in their society.

They express themselves in many ways. Body language is used to convey the rules of the pack and to establish rank. The alpha male and female are dominant and are easy to spot because of their stature; they stand erect, tall and proud, with their tails held high. They are the leaders of the pack and look undeniably confident.

Lower-ranking wolves exhibit submissive behavior by slouching lower to the ground, lowering their ears, pulling their tail between their legs or offering their throat or groin. They often greet a more dominant member of the pack with a muzzle lick to show subservience, just as a servant might kiss a king's scepter. Andrew paid close attention to the wolves' body language; it helped him anticipate their next move in the field.

Wolves also communicate with sound, and Andrew listened acutely when the wolves talked. He picked up the nuances and subtleties of their vocalizations by spending long days in the field and then reviewing hours of footage in the editing suite. He recorded their barks, howls, yips, yaps and squeals and got to know the reaction these calls evoked in specific situations.

Like their body language, the vocal exchanges revealed what was happening between pack members and helped him predict their intentions so he could follow with the camera. He had an ear for their dialect, and when he let out a howl in wolf country, his call was reciprocated with a chorus of howls and sometimes even attracted a wolf to the lens.

Andrew's next assignment was to film the mysterious "coast wolves" in the Great Bear Rainforest on the northwest coast of British Columbia. These red-ochre wolves thrived on salmon from the coastal estuaries. The shoot was to begin in September 2004, coinciding with the annual salmon spawn. Andrew had heard intriguing and ominous stories about these mysterious, salmon-eating wolves and was anxious to get near them.

He sailed up the coastline with a small crew including the producer, the captain and a Heiltsuk First Nations guide. His goal was to film the wolves as they hunted and feasted on spawning salmon, a diet that distinguished them from the rest of the world's wolf population, who dine predominately on mammals.

As they traveled along the coastline, the crew saw evidence of wolves in the area—plenty of wolf scat and salmon carcasses. The problem was finding a good location to set up a blind so he could film them without being detected.

The rain was steady and unrelenting. After a couple weeks, the crew's sprits were low. They were getting tired—and wet. Then the main camera quit because of condensation buildup. The crew turned back to get a new camera, but Andrew decided to stay on by himself. There was only one week left of the expedition, and Andrew had not yet filmed enough footage to make a documentary. He needed to capture images of the wolves hunting salmon in the estuaries and was not about to lose valuable shooting days.

He had heard there was a small island nearby where a pack of coastal wolves lived. The wolves were thought to have swum over to the island from the mainland in 1996, crossing more than nine miles of frigid ocean to get there. Apparently the pack had decimated the populations of every large mammal on the island, including deer, beaver, mink and otter. Now they gorged six months of the year on salmon and foraged on clams and tide pool life the rest of the year.

Andrew was thrilled at the opportunity to be alone with the wolves. Knowing their timid and suspicious nature, he believed this was the perfect opportunity for him to slip quietly and undetected onto the island and roll film.

The wolves were the only predators on the island, and they were the dominant species. It was a wolf's haven, a safe retreat from the interference of the outside world. Andrew had heard unsettling stories from locals living in the area about the wolves' fearless attitude toward humans.

There were several accounts of the wolves' bold, aggressive behavior. Apparently, they had surrounded and barked at a "creek walker" hired to count the salmon in the streams for the Department of Fisheries and Oceans; attacked a kayaker, biting his leg right through his tent; and closed in on a family who had come to the island to harvest clams. In the latter case, one wolf had been shot.

Andrew had never experienced any kind of aggression from wolves; they were always more afraid of him that he was of them. Rumors of their bravado interested him but did not quash his desire to spend the night on a remote island by himself. And besides, he had never heard of a death caused by a wolf attack in the wild.

When the captain dropped him on the shores of the secluded island, Andrew had only the bare essentials—a small handheld back-up camera and night vision camera, a tent, food and other supplies, a buck knife and bear spray. He would spend one night alone filming the wolves, and the crew would pick him up the next day at noon. It was early evening as he hiked through the lush maze of old growth rainforest, with red cedars towering up to 250 feet and casting ominous shadows across his path. The incessant drizzle and fog added to the gloomy atmosphere that veiled the island. He scouted the area near the estuary and found fresh salmon kills.

Andrew set up 50 feet from the water's edge on a high point that offered good sightlines to watch the wolves hunt. He pitched his small tent near the edge of the forest and wrapped a camouflage-patterned canvas around some trees and twigs to serve as a blind.

A handsome red wolf with bright gold eyes showed up at the estuary within the first hour to devour a large, pink salmon. Then he meandered through the long grasses and trotted back into the forest. The conditions were ideal for watching wolves; it was a rainy evening, which kept his scent close to the ground and helped him remain unnoticed.

A few moments passed, and the wolf returned. He had discovered Andrew's blind and tent. Andrew remained silent inside the blind as the lone wolf poked around the campsite, investigating the intruder. After a thorough snoop, he vanished into the darkness.

Andrew remembers, "It was too dark to film, and I couldn't see anything around my tent, so I decided to hunker down for the night. Within seconds of zipping my tent closed, the wolf returned. And he was not happy."

The wolf began to bark and growl outside the skimpy tent. Andrew was terrified and unsure what to do; he had never experienced anything like this before. Clutching the bear spray and the knife, he held his breath and listened. "Finally the wolf was quiet, and I assumed he was gone. I sat up most of the night listening and wondering where the wolf could be."

After a sleepless night, Andrew was greeted the next morning by "a cathedral of singing thrushes and wrens and the distant chorus of howling wolves." He headed to the blind and filmed two medium-sized wolves pluck 15- to 20-pound salmon from the water with ease.

The wolves' powerful jaws crushed the fish's skull in one bite, and then they ripped the head off to eat the brains. He was engrossed with the action, his eye glued to the camera lens, when he suddenly realized he was being watched from the edge of the trees. It appeared to be the adult who had surprised him the night before, this time with two pups at his side.

Judging from the strong stance and confident attitude, Andrew believed this chap was the alpha male. He filmed the trio for a couple hours as the pups chased each other under the watchful eye of the adult, who eventually joined in the fun. Andrew was pleased—he was finally getting some great shots of the mysterious coast wolves.

That day the crew did not show up at noon, as promised. Andrew tried unsuccessfully to contact them on the radio and realized they must be out of range. He was not in the least bit concerned. He still had food and water and, more importantly, was gathering incredible footage of the wolves.

About 20 minutes after sunset, the pack emerged from the forest to do some hunting at low tide. The alpha male, however, had another agenda and walked straight for Andrew's blind, veering off into the trees behind him. Wolves have amazing eyesight and grow more confident after dark.

Andrew used the night vision camera and filmed them poking around the tent. All of a sudden, the alpha wolf was beside the blind, just over one yard away. This was not a chance meeting; the wolf knew Andrew was there and wanted Andrew to know he knew. The wolf could see him between the twigs and canvas of the makeshift blind and was curious to check him out. Andrew kept filming.

"I shouted at the wolf to back off, and he only came closer, growling and nudging his nose toward me with obvious interest in his eyes. I was unsure of his intentions and got out my bear spay. I shouted again, and the pups began to whimper as the alpha male was making quick little motions toward me to test and challenge my nerves." The wolf won hands down—Andrew's interest in the wolf turned to panic, and his "body shivered with fear and uncertainty."

He recognized the wolf's body language from filming in the Mackenzie Bison Sanctuary. The wolves there had taunted a bison with sharp, short lunges, pressuring it to break away from the herd and run so they could chase it and take it down. A jolt of reality pierced Andrew's mind; this wolf was exhibiting predator behavior, and Andrew was the prey.

Andrew continued to film, one hand on the camera and the other clasping the pepper spray, as the wolf advanced. The wolf could easily lunge through the flimsy blind at any second. Andrew's adrenalin was pumping, and his body was in a fight-or-flight state.

He yelled again, but the wolf was not backing down. Finally, he discharged the bear spray in the wolf's face. The wind carried the spray slightly sideways, but the wolf jumped back, licking his lips. The startled pups whimpered as the male retreated and settled down with them in front of the blind.

The pups' vocalizations must have rallied the troops, because two other wolves appeared on the scene. The alpha male showed no effects from the bear spray, and the pack crept back into the forest. The night was pitch black, and Andrew could hear the wolves padding through the bush behind the tent. "They were moving all around, and I couldn't see a damn thing in the dark. I tried to use the night vision camera to find them."

He had become the watched and harassed animal. The wolves were in total control. It was impossible to spot them, and Andrew was rapidly reviewing his options, trying to decide what to do.

He was confused and caught off guard by their atypical display of aggression.

"Here I was...standing in a blind, at night, in the pouring rain. I knew I couldn't run away. They would have chased me and taken me down. I had three options: stay in the blind, try and climb a huge, slippery, wet tree or retreat to the tent. I decided the tent was my best option as they would not be able to see once I was inside."

He listened, straining to decipher the wolves' movements through the pounding rain. The brush and forest floor resonated with the packs' movement; the time to flee was now or never. He raced to his tent and, within seconds, the pack was back, close enough for Andrew to hear them breathe, anxious and expectant.

The alpha male barked and growled as he walked up to the front of the tent. Andrew understood the message: the bark was a warning signal to alert pack mates of possible danger; the growl, a distinctive, bass sound emitted from deep inside the animal, was the ultimate warning and one to be taken seriously.

Andrew was the outsider, fighting to hold his own against a pack of resident wolves. These wild dogs were not afraid to let the stranger know whose territory he was in. Andrew battled his fear, hoping for a glimmer of insight to guide him.

Instinct kicked in, and Andrew knew what to do. He needed to think like a wolf and become a wild animal, one the wolves would not want to mess with. Instead of yelling and shouting at them, he barked and growled like a wolf. He mimicked their vocalizations, injecting as much aggression and hostility into his human voice as possible.

The tactic seemed to work, and the pack left him alone after a few minutes. His senses were heightened and his nerves were frayed. He could feel their presence as they wandered the surrounding forest.

"Cones would fall from the Sitka spruce giants and bounce off the roof of my tent, sending a shot of adrenalin straight to my heart. It eased my nerves a little once I could hear the wolves howling a short distance away in the estuary. At least I knew where they were now, and they were not concentrating on me."

It was another sleepless night for Andrew. The wolves hunted salmon all night and visited his camp more than once, this time ignoring him. He had used his wits and experience to prevent what could have been a fatal encounter. Andrew was hoping the crew would show up soon.

He continued to film the next morning, determined to gather more footage. The wolves were scattered throughout the estuary, gnawing on salmon and playing. They seemed oblivious to him as he filmed from the blind. Andrew believed that they had started to accept him or at least tolerate his presence.

At one point, the alpha male deliberately killed a salmon but didn't eat it. Instead, he carried it from the estuary and threw it down in front of the blind. Andrew wasn't sure if the wolf was leaving an offering or sending a message of his power, strength and agility, but he was thankful for the truce.

This small step toward harmony was fortuitous because the sun was setting and there was still no sign of the crew. Andrew continued to shoot into the evening and, once again, the pack returned. The alpha male was back at the blind showing antagonism and agitation.

Andrew spoke in a deep, gentle voice. "Hey, how are you doing? Settle down. It's okay, let's be friends." The wolf paused to listen and then left to go about his business.

The crew finally radioed later that night. They had been delayed trying to replace the camera. Andrew filled them in on his frightening ordeal, and they assured him they were on their way.

The sight of his "rescuers" clomping down the beach at midnight, outfitted in hip waders and armed with canoe paddles, was comic relief to the tension that had built up over the last two days. He was relieved to spend the night off the wolves' island and back on the sailboat.

Andrew never anticipated that "speaking wolf" would help him survive his terrifying experience. The footage he gathered for the documentary, *Secrets of the Coast Wolf*, was spectacular, and the trip was a success.

He still dreams of the expedition and is filled with mixed emotion—a sense of awe as he remembers the wolves playing and greeting each other with wagging tails, and a hint of dread as they closed in on him. "I still look back and recall the close encounters I had with these wolves. I have to say, I would do it again in a heartbeat."

~∞~

Creature Feature

Wolves are considered one of the most intelligent of all land predators and are at least 10 times more intelligent than the smartest dogs. They can smell prey up to 1.75 miles away, hear up to six miles in the forest and 10 miles in the open and have a reflective retina that makes their night vision excellent. Their jaws exert twice as much pressure as those of a German shepherd. Adult wolves have no natural predators, except for humans.

CHAPTER ELEVEN

Zoo Tales

An animal's eyes have the power to speak a great language.

—Martin Buber

AS A CHILD, I ENVIED zookeepers. Imagine being able to train tigers, feed monkeys or have an owl perch on your arm. What a joy!

As an adult, my interest did not wane. So I applied at the Edmonton Valley Zoo to work as a volunteer for the primate collection. I was so excited that I couldn't sleep the night before my first shift. All I could think about was how amazing it was going to be to feed the bright-eyed lemurs and be around all those animals. I couldn't believe my luck!

Several years later I became a zookeeper at the same zoo and learned that loving animals was as important a component as commitment and diligence to a job that was often strenuous, dirty and smelly. Caring for animals is a lot of hard work. Zookeepers are outside in all weather, and much like the postman, "neither snow, nor rain, nor heat, nor night" keeps them from completing their rounds. The animals eat every day, so zookeepers work 365 days a year.

And did I mention that wild animals can bite, kick and claw? Zookeepers know that these animals are not domesticated pets; there is always a chance for unpredictable behavior.

Zookeepers understand the human-animal bond intimately. They devote their lives to caring for animals, striving to ensure the animals are healthy, happy and living with dignity in their zoo home. Each day, zookeepers work and breathe alongside these clawed, pawed, winged and finned beings.

Over time, they get to know the animals and their unique personalities. Relationships are explored and bonds are developed. The keepers deal with living, feeling, responding beings; the job does not end when the shift is over. They are dedicated to caring for these animals, and sometimes they make personal sacrifices, all for the love of the animal.

Going Ape

It was a bitterly cold winter morning on Sunday, December 9, 2007, so hauling myself out of a warm, toasty bed to get ready for my 7:00 AM shift at the Edmonton Valley Zoo should have a been a challenge. Instead, I popped up at 5:30 AM and raced off to work. Julia, the white-handed gibbon, was pregnant and expecting her seventh baby any day. So, my first piece of business was to check on the expectant mother. One of these mornings, I knew, there was going to be a tiny baby clinging to her belly.

Keeping to my routine, I headed down to her enclosure to peek through the window. Julia was sitting quietly on a branch and her mate, Chan, was not far away. At first glance, all appeared well, but when I took a closer look at Julia, I could see there was something wrong. Dangling down between her legs was a tiny hand. I radioed my supervisor right away so the veterinarian could be contacted.

Julia's baby was obviously facing the wrong direction. As we waited for the veterinarian to arrive, we crossed our fingers, hoping the baby would right itself and Julia would deliver naturally, just as she had her other six babies. At least this unborn infant was alive—every so often its little hand would open and close, making a fist.

The veterinarian arrived and knew immediately that an emergency Cesarean section was the only hope. The surgery was a success, and a little ape named Penelope entered the world. The umbilical cord had been wrapped around the baby's neck twice, so there was no possibility of a natural birth. Pregnancy complications occur in the wild, but neither baby nor mom would have survived this situation without medical intervention.

Penelope's birth weight was just less than one pound, which was healthy indeed. Julia and her baby were placed in a cozy crate to sleep, where the veterinarian could keep a close eye on them. That first night, Penelope managed to swallow some nutrient-rich first milk, the colostrum, and was bottle-fed formula as mama slept after her surgery.

The next morning, the veterinarian watched Julia to monitor her health, as well as that of the baby. It was crucial that the newborn was nursing and was being cradled in her mother's arms. Julia was allowing the baby to suckle, but was not encouraging her to do so, nor was she embracing the baby to keep the tiny, hairless body warm. It was possible that Julia was still a little woozy from the anesthetic and sore from the surgery. She did, after all, have stitches running up her belly from the C-section, exactly where Penelope needed to cling to suckle.

It was possible that the bonding process would take a little longer because of Julia's surgery. Until they were sure that Penelope was getting enough nutrition from mom, she would have to be bottle-fed and weighed daily to monitor her development. Penelope spent the day with mom, but Julia seemed disinterested in her, and the zookeepers observed almost no feeding. Another decision had to be made—Penelope could not be left overnight without guaranteed food and warmth from her mother.

So that night, zookeeper Andi Sime took Penelope home. Andi didn't have kids of her own, but she did have a three-year-old baby sister and a lot of practice babysitting during her youth. Raised on a farm in Fort Saskatchewan, Alberta, Andi's babysitting experience also ventured into the farmyard, where she assisted her father with the delivery and care of newborn calves. Her studies in Developmental Psychology at the University of Alberta also came in handy because human and primate babies are very similar.

The zoo's veterinarian monitored Penelope's health and worked with Andi, adjusting the diet as the infant developed. Her co-workers offered to babysit and share their experience and knowledge with her, making the prospect of raising a baby ape a little less daunting.

Andi felt as equipped as anyone could with a ward that is a newborn ape. It was critical that Penelope was bottle-fed formula every three hours on the dot and that she was kept warm. The first feeding took 45 minutes, and Penelope drank only the tiniest amount of milk, about one tablespoon.

The rest of the evening was devoted to the challenge of diapers. What does one put on a baby ape? Andi experimented with bits of cloth and finally settled on preemie baby diapers altered to fit.

Warmth was a big concern because Penelope was basically hairless. She needed to be at 98.6°F to 100.4°F at all times. Andi bundled Penelope in fleece blankets, placed her in a snuggly and then strapped it to her own body. Where Andi went,

Penelope went. Andi was not letting this tiny 35-hour-old ape out of her sight.

Next, a makeshift crib for sleeping. A laundry basket ended up being perfect. Once the basket was padded with soft blankets and a heating pad, Penelope was set for the night; all she needed was a teddy bear and a soother. It was an anxious first night for Andi, not to mention sleepless, as she dutifully got up every three hours to feed the hungry infant, change her diapers and settle her back to sleep. Little did Andi know that this was only the beginning....

For the next week, Penelope was reintroduced to her ape mother each day. Julia was recovering nicely from her surgery, but when Penelope was put in the enclosure, the ape mother simply ignored her. The maternal instincts that had allowed Julia to raise six other healthy babies did not kick in. Penelope would never survive under these circumstances. She needed to be hand raised, and Andi volunteered to become Penelope's primary caretaker. And so that first evening's "trial run" became the daily routine for the next seven months. Andi was about to learn what it meant to be a mother.

Andi was excited, anxious and emotional all at the same time. "I had total mama jitters. I was so nervous. If she slept too deeply, I would check her. If she cried, I would check her. I checked her all the time and worried a lot." Andi kept a careful log of Penelope's daily weight, how much she ate, her physical development and her behavior. She boiled bottles, changed diapers, did loads of laundry, gave baths and cuddled and cooed, as mamas do.

Almost immediately, Andi and Penelope became one. Penelope was strapped to her throughout the day and accompanied her to work. Andi worked the late afternoon shift in the zoo's commissary, preparing the animals' diets and doing the evening rounds. The rest of the day was devoted to Penelope and all of her needs.

Andi called her a "bundle of instincts"; Penelope knew how to grasp but other than that had no mobility on her own. In nature, she would have clung tightly to her mother's underside. The mother would have added support with her strong arms and tucked her knees up to embrace the baby when swinging from tree to tree. Luckily, Andi didn't have to worry about the swinging part!

As the days passed, Andi became more confident and relaxed; the baby and her surrogate mom had settled into a routine, and things were going well. Penelope was gaining weight, growing hair and acting much like a human baby. When she wanted attention or was hungry, she cried and fussed.

Andi's personal life changed radically. You can't exactly go to the gym or hang out at the pub with a small ape strapped to your chest. And she was getting tired with the nightly feedings every three hours, but the relationship between her and

Penelope was deepening. "It was so strange at first, not going out. This little entity was attached to me all day long. My entire day—home and work routine—revolved around her. Everywhere I went, I had a diaper bag. She took over my life."

At two months, Penelope was starting to extend her arms and explore things. Two of the things she explored were Andi's family pets, Ding the cat and Fraise the dog. The palms of Penelope's hands and the soles of her feet are smooth and free of fur, making them sensitive, and she has opposable thumbs, which allow her to easily grasp objects.

Penelope, a baby white-handed gibbon, hugs her teddy.

"Penelope started by grabbing the ears of the animals and enjoying the sensation of their fur. It was about touching and feeling. Then she would lay her hands on their heads and finally go in for a whole body cuddle."

As Penelope grew, her big, round, chocolate brown eyes became increasingly alert and inquisitive. The gibbon, like the gorilla or chimpanzee, is an ape, not a monkey; it does not have a tail, and its brain is larger.

One day Andi attended a baby shower. She hadn't socialized in a long while and was looking forward to seeing her friends. The rules were quite strict when it came to Penelope; no one else could hold her or touch her. At one point during the afternoon, the guests played a game. They were asked to sample a variety of baby foods arranged on a plate and then identify them. The plate came around to Andi, and before she knew it Penelope had swiped her hand through the food. Without thinking, Andi grabbed the ape's long slender hand and licked off the baby food. Silence fell over the room and jaws dropped. Now we've all seen a mother do this with her baby, but it takes a moment to register when the hand belongs to an ape. Andi laughs now reflecting on that moment. "She becomes your own and you don't even think about it."

By six months, Penelope was eating solid foods and starting to explore and show mobility on her own. She was still sleeping in her laundry basket,

Penelope and zookeeper mom, Andi, enjoy a snuggle together.

swathed in blankets and attached to a teddy, but that was about to change. One night, Andi woke up having trouble breathing. As her senses cleared and the fogginess of sleep lifted, she realized the problem. She had an ape on her face. Penelope had crawled out of her basket and decided to join mom in the big bed. After that, it was tough keeping Penelope in her basket for the night.

When Penelope was seven months old, it was time to reintroduce her to her real mom, Julia. She needed to learn how to act like an ape and observe ape behaviors such as grooming, playing, foraging for food and the appropriate social behavior. And, she needed to learn how to "sing." The white-handed gibbon is distinguished by its musical howl. Although it is generally quiet during the day, the gibbon often howls at sunrise and sunset, making loud "whoop" sounds. To this day, when Penelope sees Andi, she acknowledges her with a friendly gibbon-style greeting—the corners of Penelope's mouth are drawn back, revealing the teeth, and there's a whole lot of chatter.

Andi gave Penelope seven months of love, care and devotion. I asked Andi what Penelope gave her. She said, "Confidence. The prospect of raising an ape is mind-boggling. There is no manual. It was a blessing to be so intimately involved with her life. Yes, it was an unnatural bond, but it was an honor. It was very intimate, being her primary caretaker, being the one, being her mom. The fabric of her life and mine were totally intertwined."

Armed and Dangerous!

Most marine biologists agree the octopus is the most intelligent of all invertebrates; some even compare its intelligence to that of a house cat. This eight-armed wonder is equipped with a large brain, a highly developed nervous system and a good memory, making it trainable and capable of solving difficult puzzles and mazes. Its strong, flexible arms, lined with rows of suckers for gripping, are extremely sensitive to touch. And the octopus has amazing eyesight. Hmmm...sounds like trouble to me.

Many aquariums housing octopuses have reported their mischievous and inquisitive nature, noting that they like to play. To keep the creatures stimulated, the staff offers an assortment of toys and games with which they can amuse themselves. As the old saying goes, "a busy octopus is a happy octopus." With big brains and curious personalities, these playful cephalopods can wreak havoc when they have too much time on their hands...rather *arms*.

Back in the 1990s, the staff at San Francisco's Steinhart Aquarium suspected the night engineer when Dungeness crabs started disappearing from their tank. But eyes turned to the octopus when crab shells began appearing at the bottom of its tank. All suspicions were confirmed when the engineer found an octopus in the hallway one night. It turned out that this crab-craving octopus was crawling out of its tank and into the crab tank for a feast whenever the urge hit.

Mystery struck again, this time at the Sea Star Aquarium in Coburg, Germany. The aquarium is closed weekdays during the winter season. Without the hubbub of visitors, it is unusually quiet and still, and one of its occupants was showing the signs of a disgruntled and bored toddler.

Otto, a two-foot, seven-inch-long, six-month-old octopus was twiddling his eight arms and looking for some action. This rambunctious octopus loved to play, and the staff had taught him how to aim and squirt water at the visitors. The game amused Otto, and he enjoyed interacting with his damp admirers.

When the aquarium closed for its winter hours, Otto was not happy and let the staff know it. As reported by *The Daily Telegraph*, Director Elfriede Kummer said: "Once we saw him juggling the hermit crabs in his tank; another time he threw stones against the glass, damaging it. And from time to time, he completely rearranges his tank to make it suit his own taste better—much to the distress of his fellow tank inhabitants."

Otto even confiscated scrubbers from the staff when they were cleaning the inside of his exhibit, and decided not to return them. Hey, he's got eight arms. Who's going to argue?

One night toward the end of October 2008, the aquarium's electrical system shorted out, cutting off the power to all the tanks. Electricians fixed it first thing in the morning, but then it happened the next night...and the next. The electricians were baffled and could find no explanation for the power outages. It was a serious matter—turning off every filter and water pump in the building put the lives of all the animals at risk.

On the third night, the staff decided to camp out and take shifts sleeping on the floor to try to find out what was causing these puzzling blackouts. No one saw anything out of the ordinary. It wasn't until Elfriede arrived the next morning that she witnessed not *what*...but rather *who* was responsible for the chaos. Otto had crawled to the edge of his tank and with a carefully directed a jet of water squirted the spotlight that hung above him, short-circuiting the light.

Several newspaper articles incorrectly suggested that the light was too bright and annoyed the clever cephalopod. Aquarium staff confirmed that they use special aquarium lights that are not too intense. As well, Otto's exhibit has dark overhangs and caves to which he can retreat.

"We've put the light a bit higher now so he shouldn't be able to reach it. But Otto is constantly craving for attention and always comes up with new stunts, so we have realized we will have to keep a more careful eye on him—and also perhaps give him a few more toys to play with."

Now the staff is busy thinking up ways to keep Otto occupied over the winter months. Knowing that octopuses have amazing powers of camouflage and can quickly change their color to adapt to their background, the staff gave Otto a black-and-white-checkered chessboard, hoping this difficult pattern would be hard to mimic. Otto was engaged for a while but then lost interest and tossed the board right out of his aquarium.

This multi-limbed youngster with the big personality has his keepers on their toes. The aquarium staff encourages the public to email any novel ideas or toy suggestion that might keep young Otto occupied. I say drop a Rubik's Cube into his tank. That should keep him tied up for while.

Little Blue Eyes

Some folks are cat people and some are dog people. It doesn't mean that cat people don't like dogs, but if they had their druthers, they'd spend their time with a cat. Zookeeper Wade Krasnow fancied cats.

Raised on a farm, Wade had reared and cared for a wide assortment of animals, from goats to peacocks, but cats were always his favorite. He admired their beauty and grace, loved their mischievous ways and respected their independence. Wade enjoyed spending time with his cats and always looked forward to curling up with them at the end of the day.

When the Edmonton Valley Zoo's female cougar gave birth to two cubs on October 6, 1990, Wade was ecstatic. He recalls, "The cougar was my favorite animal ever since I was a kid. Whenever I saw them on television I thought they looked so beautiful." Wade had been a zookeeper for only a couple years, so this was pure excitement.

This female cougar was historically a poor mother. She tended to over-groom her cubs (or kittens), accidentally injuring them in the process. The staff closely monitored her behavior with the babies and after 48 hours decided to pull the newborn kittens from her enclosure.

Someone was needed immediately to take on the strenuous task of hand-raising the pair of cubs. Wade volunteered on the spot. He was still living on his family's farm in the small town of Onoway, Alberta, and was sure his parents wouldn't mind another set of paws or two running about.

The kittens were tiny and looked much like domestic kittens, only a little larger. "They were these little brown-spotted fur balls. They didn't even weigh a pound, and their eyes were still closed." It was love at first sight. Wade couldn't wait to begin his role as a surrogate "mother."

Baby animals spark in many of us humans the innate urge to nurture. They tug on our natural instincts to protect the vulnerable, and as a result, a flood of good feeling and joy rushes in and we experience a kind of baby love.

Wade's entry into parenthood was abrupt— these babies needed to be fed every four hours, and if they weren't, there was a whole lot of meowing and complaining. For a young man in his twenties, this daily schedule certainly restricted his social life, but Wade took on the role eagerly and bonded quickly with his furry wards. He named the little girl Sheena and the boy Chinook.

Wade bottle-fed them a formula of milk replacement and protein powder. They had hearty appetites and drank greedily. So far so good—feeding was going to be a breeze. Of course, there were two of them, so that was going to take a little extra time because Wade could only manage one at a time.

Then there was the matter of stimulating them to urinate and defecate before or after each feeding. A mother cat normally licks her kitten's bottom to encourage them to release their bladder and bowel. Wade decided the easiest and cleanest method would be to hold each cub over the sink or toilet, run the tap with warm water, and then using a wet finger stroke the area until he achieved the desired results.

The first time he tried stimulating the twins to do their "business," he was a little nervous. Raising these cubs was a huge responsibility, and he wanted everything to go perfectly. When the first trip to the loo was successful, Wade said, "I was never so happy to see poop!" Like a new parent with a baby, he wanted to shout "whoopee" every time a bathroom break was successful.

The first couple weeks were pretty much about eating, eliminating and sleeping. He transported them to and from work in a travel crate, keeping them in a quiet room at work and in his bedroom at home. These two squirmy kittens had taken over his life. It was like being a single dad with twins... and he loved it.

The cubs slept in a cozy crate warmed with a heating pad and blankets. The veterinarian checked them weekly and was happy with their progress. The cubs were gaining weight and were healthy. Wade was a getting a little tired with the midnight and 4:00 AM feedings, but it was all worth it.

A couple weeks later, the kittens opened their eyes. Wade's heart melted as two sets of bright blue eyes looked up at him. The eyes remain blue for about 16 months and then change to a greenish yellow.

As the weeks passed, the twins started to play and behaved much like domestic cats. They kneaded their paws on his hands, chased a string around the room and squirmed and yowled when he tickled their stomach. Now when he fed these bouncing babies, their claws firmly gripped his hand and dug in if he dared to remove the bottle before they were done. His scratched arms were evidence of their rambunctious romps and a reminder that these wild cats were not house pets.

The cubs wrestled with each other and took turns pouncing on Wade. The bond was getting stronger between the twins and their caretaker. The three spent a lot of time playing, cuddling and hanging out together. The cubs responded to their names and to Wade's voice.

He was a devoted papa and stressed and fussed like new parents do. Were they getting enough to eat? Why did they shed some fur? One time the pair had a bout of diarrhea after solid food was introduced. The veterinarian assured him everything was fine, but that didn't stop him from going to the library to do research and calling other zoos.

"I felt so responsible for their lives and I did whatever I could to keep them healthy. You have the same feelings for a child…you want to protect them. These were my children."

As the cubs grew, Wade started to exercise them outside. He took them for runs in a protected area of the zoo. That was one of their favorite activities to blow off some energy. They were also vocal. There was the "I need you right away" meow and the "bring that bottle back" growl and a long purr when they were content. Cougars are, in fact, the largest purring cats.

The twins were doing great, and the zoo curator told Wade that they were ready to live at the zoo full time. Wade knew this day was coming and had tried to prepare for it.

"It was hard to let go at first because they are with you 24 hours a day. The first night they spent at the zoo, I lay awake wondering 'Are they okay? Do they miss me?'" The next day he checked, and of course, the cubs were fine. Wade was experiencing "empty nest syndrome" and knew that it would take time to pass.

The cougar cubs continued to grow, and three months later, Chinook was transferred to another zoo. Wade tried to convince the curator to keep Sheena, but a little male cougar was waiting to keep her company in Winnipeg, Manitoba. This would be the best place for her. Sheena was to be sent in two weeks.

Wade and Sheena spent as much time together as possible before her departure. He loved her company, and she returned the affection. Their bond was tight. He was sad that she was leaving, and he would likely never see her again.

The day she left, they went for long run together through the snow. Then he gave her a teary hug before sending her on her way. "It was like sending your child off to college," he recalls.

Two years later, Wade visited the zoo in Winnipeg "to see my baby." He spotted her in a large enclosure with her mate and called out her name. Sheena came right up to the front of the enclosure, faced him and purred. He was happy to see her.

Almost 20 years later, Wade still thinks about his time with the baby cougars. "It was a privilege to be able to get so close to one of Mother Nature's creatures—fellow inhabitants of the world. To have something impact your life like that, you grow more gentle. They soothe your soul."

Wade is now the head of Animal Care at the Edmonton Valley Zoo and has cared for many different species of local and exotic animals. His time with the cougar cubs will always be his most powerful and memorable encounter.

⁓❀⁓

Creature Feature

The cougar, also known as a mountain lion or puma, is the largest wild cat in North America. It is a successful predator with supreme agility. Its powerful hind legs can propel the cat 30 to 45 feet forward, and it can jump 18 feet upward from a sitting position. The cougar sprints 40 miles per hour and can also swim. Humans are the cougar's only predator.

CHAPTER TWELVE

Magical Marine Moments

Lots of people talk to animals...Not very many listen, though...That's the problem.

—Benjamin Hoff, *The Tao of Pooh*

THE OCEAN COVERS ALMOST three-quarters of the planet's surface, yet it remains one of the Earth's last unexplored frontiers. This vast undersea world, squirming with strange creatures, has stirred imaginations for millennia. Myths of mermaids and sea monsters are hard to dismiss when scientists continue to discover new, bizarre species: corals that fluoresce in the dark, giant sea spiders running along the ocean floor and prehistoric-looking armored fish.

Not long ago, a trawler caught a 28-foot-long giant squid, once thought to be a "sea serpent," off the coast of the Falkland Islands. This 10-limbed creature emerged from the ocean's abyss 3300 feet below the surface—yet another humbling reminder that we have a lot left to learn.

Fish are one of the oldest life forms on Earth, believed to have emerged 500 million years ago. To put this in perspective, humans have only been walking the planet for around 200,000 years. Compared to the ancient life that exists in the sea, we are the new kids on the block. There are many unexplained mysteries, and perhaps this is what entices us to explore the underwater world.

Scuba diving opened the door for us land dwellers to explore the fantastical world beneath the ocean's surface, an underwater utopia rich with weird and wonderful creatures.

Chances are good that you remember the first time you explored a tide pool or plunged into the sea to snorkel or dive. For Scott Jackson, his first open water dive had such a profound affect on him that it shaped the direction of his life.

Scott traveled to Hawaii in February 1988 to complete his Open Water Diver course. His first dive as a bona fide certified scuba diver was at First Cathedral, an amazing site off of Lanai Island, Maui. It is a large lava tube, approximately 100 feet long and two stories tall, that looks like a church, complete with an arched doorway, choir balcony and even a "stained glass window," an effect produced by the light being reflected off the crystal blue water. The dive ended with Scott swimming out a "side door" and coming face to face with a spiny balloon-shaped puffer fish. What a dive!

Scott and his dive buddies surfaced and climbed back into the boat for a quick snack before their next dive. He was thrilled with his first experience and eternally grateful that he was no longer a snorkeler, trapped in the shallows. Obviously, he was still an air-breathing visitor, but now he could venture down to much greater depths and stay a while to explore and take in the magic.

The group was exchanging stories when they spotted two adult humpback whales with a little one in between. Hawaiian myth claims that the whale is a manifestation of the Hawaiian god, Kanaloa—the god of the ocean. Scott couldn't believe his eyes...or his luck.

"They just started hanging out near the boat. The laws protecting these animals are very strict, and humans are not allowed to approach them, but they can approach humans if they choose."

Scott grabbed his fins, snorkel and mask and hopped into the water. The baby was about 10 feet long, making it one or two days old. The mother stayed beneath the baby keeping a close eye on the situation with the auntie by her side. The adults were huge; they can measure 45 to 50 feet long and weigh up to 40 tons, making a huge impression on a mask-clad human.

The calf was curious, as babies are, and decided to swim forward to take a closer peek at these two-legged creatures. The mother looked on showing no fear and put Scott at total ease. Scott looked at the mother and auntie and was lost in their expressions; he believed he was alongside gentle giants.

The baby continued to approach, nudging closer to Scott until it was only 10 feet away. It was an indescribable experience and quite unexpected. Then, Scott looked directly into the whale's eye.

"The eye was huge, the size of a softball. When I looked at it, it was like looking into a mirror. I saw a human eye—the color, the depth, the movement. It had a human expression. I could tell there was thought and a lot of stuff happening in there."

Scott hung in the water for what seemed like a long time as the whales checked him and the group out. "As I watched them, I could feel their curiosity and innocence. But it was the eyes—you know how fish eyes are just that, sort of flat with no depth to them, but the whale's eyes—they were looking into you, not at you. It was completely overwhelming."

It was an amazing encounter to happen just out of the blue, and of course, it sealed the deal. Scott was absolutely hooked on diving. But the experience also dramatically changed the course of his career and his life.

"It changed me from a recreational diver and drove me to go much further. I quit my job in Canada and moved to Catalina Island, California, to work on a dive charter and teach. It was there that I become a Master Scuba Diver Trainer. My life was all about diving. I lived and worked on a boat."

Science will never be able to explain what Scott experienced in that life-changing moment. "I've been diving 21 years now, and it was the best day of diving I have ever had. There was such a connection with the whales. What a privilege for me to have had that encounter."

Hello Sucker!

Inger Sheil had been exploring tide pools near her home in Bungan Beach, Newport, Australia, near Sydney, since she was a child. The rock pools were full of life: crabs, fish, snails and sometimes even octopuses.

Octopuses were especially fascinating to her, and it's not hard to see why. What other creature has a soft blob for a body that is capable of changing color, texture and shape; eight long, suckered, arms branching directly from the head that curl and twist like the hair of Medusa; a beak for killing prey and injecting venom; and the ability to shoot black ink? Octopuses have all the elements needed for a horror movie, which no doubt inspired Jules Verne when penning his famous novel, *20,000 Leagues Under The Sea*.

The first "occie" (a nickname for octopuses "down under") Inger ever saw was resting in a shallow pool. Her father used a net to gently scoop it out and release it into the sea because he was concerned that it was too exposed to people and may be harmed. This first mindful encounter began her lifelong interest in octopuses.

As a youngster, Inger didn't really know how to relate to an octopus. "They fascinated me, but I was too rough and boisterous in my approaches, poking and trying to touch, and they would shrink deep into their crevasses until nary an eye or a tentacle could be seen."

Exercising caution when it comes to handling local octopods is a good thing; Sydney is home to the famous "blue-ringed octopus," recognized as being one of the most venomous creatures on Earth. Though only the size of a golf ball, this octopus has a poison that will kill a human within minutes, and there is no known antidote. So it always pays to check out the rock pools before wading about and to be careful when picking up large shells or bottles where this shy, docile creature might be living.

Extensive collecting in the '80s took its toll on the rock pool inhabitants, and Inger's tide pool excursions revealed far less animal life than she had observed as a small child in Bungan Beach— the large crabs were gone, and there were, sadly, comparatively few occies to spot.

"As an adult, I never lost my love of critters but learned to be much calmer around them and to let them approach me to interact." Inger learned to dive in 1996 and loved to spend time around cephalopods, including squid, cuttlefish and octopuses.

"We have many cuttlefish around Sydney, and they always amuse me, hovering under their overhangs, looking like wise old men with hooded eyes and beards. There are darting squid to be seen as well, but by far my favorites are the occies."

Inger figured out that the best way to approach one of these shy, elusive creatures was to find its den, then quietly rest a hand outside it. Once an octopus finishes eating, he sweeps his den clean, pushing the empty crab and snail shells into a pile outside the opening. Inger found that slowly moving the shells around from its "octopus garden" could sometimes attract the occie's interest. If she was fortunate, she would be rewarded with an arm or two rolling out of the dark den, curious to touch her skin and wrap around her hand.

One afternoon in the Australian summer of 1997–98, Inger decided to wander down to the nearby beach for a dip. Bungan was a great beach to visit and was never too crowded. It was a bit challenging to get to, surrounded with high cliffs and accessible only via a steep path. Because it was low tide, she decided to have a poke around the rock pools after the dip.

"I had a feeling it was a good day for finding interesting things like nudibranchs, juvenile exotic fish riding the currents from the tropical north, crabs and bits and bobs." She wasn't surprised when, wandering near the edge of the natural rock platform, she saw something interesting at the bottom of a small pool. The pool was cut off from direct contact with the sea at low tide but would have been well covered when the tide was in.

Closer inspection revealed an octopus with rusty red coloration on the undersides of its arms. He (or she) was a Common Sydney octopus, also known as the gloomy octopus. This is the largest octopus commonly seen in Sydney and grows to about 31.5 inches; this specimen was about half that size.

"Extremely pleased, I sat down to observe the octopus, which had shrunk almost all the way back into his den at the bottom of the pool when he saw me. I decided to try and introduce myself and slipped my hand into the pool."

He watched Inger and after a minute or two, cautiously approached, stretching out a few of his arms to gently check out her hand. Gaining a bit of courage, he cautiously crept farther from his den and approached the surface. Inger watched as he snaked two arms back into the deeper part of the pool and anchored them firmly in his den. Once he was satisfied, the lightly touching arm tips dancing along her hand tightened their grip, as he attempted to haul his catch back into his den.

This octopus had clearly met his first "penta"-pus and was planning to further investigate the appendage and all its five digits. He continued to pull, determined to have it, but Inger was not about to give up possession of her hand, so he fled back to his den. "If an octopus could be said to be in high dudgeon, he was."

After repeating the antics a few more times, Inger decide to change tack. She walked over to the base of the cliffs where small crabs take up residence under rocks, caught one and returned to the pool. "I had the occie's undivided attention. When I dropped the crab in, he leapt on it with a swift, undulating pounce, blanching his color almost white as he did so."

And so began their unique friendship. Inger christened him Cthulu, after the multi-tentacled character created by horror author H.P. Lovecraft in 1926. "I visited Cthulu almost every day at low tide, bringing him his tribute of crabs. At first he would take the offering and retreat back to his den, but eventually he didn't bother to do so." It seemed his tendency to retreat and eagerness to pull her hand down into his den had been replaced with curiosity.

Inger would put her hand in the water, and Cthulu would crawl all over it with his tactile arms. She could feel his mouth, or beak, brushing against her skin, but he never tried to bite. He seemed genuinely curious. He was also probably sampling the goods—octopus suckers have a special chemical receptor that allows the animal to taste what it is touching. Apparently, Inger wasn't on the menu.

When Inger arrived at the edge of his rock pool, Cthulu would quickly change color, and sometimes the texture of his skin would transform from spiky to smooth or vice versa. Then he would trundle up to the surface of the pool, his long, soft arms rolling on the surface in greeting.

This continued for many weeks, and Inger became concerned that he was becoming too tame. Although it was illegal to collect on the rock platforms, some poaching did take place. She was horrified one day when, while sitting on a large rock at the base of the cliff, she saw a group of teens come across Cthulu's rock pool. "Look! An octopus!" they hollered.

Inger watched nervously. When she heard, "Let's catch him!" and jokes about occies on the "barbie," she raced to the scene.

She explained that he was a tame octopus, which may not be in his best interest. Inger showed them how he ate crabs. They were clearly amused and asked if he was her octopus. She replied that she didn't think anyone owned a wild animal, but that she was fond of this one.

They were entertained by Chtulu's crab pouncing exhibition and his instant color changes. Inger and the teens talked about octopus intelligence; the octopus has the largest brain of any invertebrate as well as excellent eyesight. Inger lingered until long after the group had left the beach and she knew Cthulu was safe.

Their daily encounters continued over the next few weeks. Cthulu greeted Inger with a suckered arm, trailing the tip ever so gently across her hand, and Inger delivered crabs. "Then suddenly, one day, Cthulu was gone when I arrived, crab in hand, to see him. I was surprised he'd stayed as long as he did—octopods are usually much more transitory and leave after a day or two."

She checked the pool frequently on her visits to the beach and worried that perhaps he'd been caught, but she believed he'd probably just decided one high tide to move on. Inger continues to look for octopuses when she is down at the beach, hoping to repeat the unique connection she shared with Cthulu. She did meet another octopus one day that decided to take up residence in Cthulu's den, but this one was much shyer and never offered more than a "single tentacle handshake."

Finally, during the summer of 2008–09 she met an octopus with an outgoing, inquisitive personality comparable to that of Cthulu. She was standing in the middle of a large, shallow rock pool, pointing out the colorful fish to her small nephews and niece when she felt something sticky winding around her ankle. "I looked down, and there was an octopus wrapping himself around my leg!" He was gregarious and curious, grabbing and pulling at hands, waving his arms about to say "g'day." It was a pleasant surprise.

Inger still checks Cthulu's pool every time she visits. "It was a great experience. And even now, many years later, with much time spent at the same beach and diving all over the world, I still regard it as one of the most memorable encounters I've ever had with a marine animal."

Touched by an Angel

Scuba divers descend from around the world to experience the warm, turquoise Caribbean waters of Utila, one of the Bay Islands off Honduras. Utila is connected to the Mesoamerican Barrier Reef, the second largest reef in the world after the Great Barrier Reef in Australia. The area is rich with diverse sea life, earning its well-deserved reputation for world-class coral reef diving. It was the ideal place for Danny Cole to learn how to scuba dive.

Danny went off to Utila in 2006 to become a certified diver and became hooked on the sport. He loved the weightless sensation of being under-water and was mesmerized with the marine life, surreal in their shape and color. This undersea world was wildly different from anything he had ever imagined. It was like being invited into a secret civilization and offered a privileged peek into another dimension of life.

He logged as many dives as he could, eager to witness this weird and wonderful world through his mask. It was easy to become entranced by the activities of the fish, darting in and out of the coral, or a large sea turtle cutting through the water, flippers beating like the wings of a bird.

He went back to Utila the following year for an extended stay. After several weeks of exceptional diving among schools of rainbow-colored fish, lobsters and octopuses, Danny had an encounter with a marine being, one that delivered a powerful message to him.

It was a hot, sunny day in paradise. Danny and his buddy had gone for a morning dive and decided to explore a nearby bay with their snorkel gear that afternoon. They waded through the shallow water until they hit the first sandbar after which the bottom dropped down 30 to 50 feet.

Nearby was another snorkeler floating on the surface; he was still and focused. Danny got a little closer to see what he was looking at and was pleasantly surprised to see a large spotted eagle ray.

This elegant ray, which is actually a flattened type of fish, is regarded as one of the most beautiful, with a dramatic design of white dots covering the dark-colored dorsal side of its smooth body. The ventral surface is snow white, making the ray easy to spot underwater as it swims. Rays swim quite differently than other fish; they move through the water with powerful wing-like pectoral fins that flap and undulate, breaking intermittently to glide.

The ray was large, its wingspan more than 4 feet across, and it looked as though it weighed more than 200 pounds. It slowly angled toward them, glimpses of white from beneath the "wings" flashing through the water with each flap. Danny hovered on the surface spellbound as he watched the animal approach.

Danny remembers, "It was right there in front of us. I'd never seen a spotted eagle ray before, but I knew instinctively that this was not something to be afraid of." They watched for about five minutes as the ray slid gracefully through the water; the boys then decided to swim down to try and get a closer look. This species of ray is typically shy and wary of divers, and though it did not let them get too close before "flying" off, it was near enough for Danny to get a good look at its features.

"The ray had a face! It had a snout that projected out like a dolphin's beak, only flatter, and these two large eyes. When I saw it, I knew immediately that it was important. It was like an angel of light with its wings spread out and gave off this peaceful energy."

Like a magician, the ray came back again a few minutes later from the opposite direction. Once again, Danny was transfixed with the face. "It had a sense of knowingness and was at such peace with the world. I felt like it was saying to me, 'Too bad you have all disconnected yourselves from the world and destroyed so much. Because of *you*, we will be the biggest losers.'" The ray swam off again, its long, whip-like tail trailing behind.

The ray came back a third time from a different direction. "It would just come out of nowhere. You knew exactly who was in control without it being contentious. I knew there was nothing to be afraid of. It was almost like it felt sorry for me."

His encounter with the ray was haunting and humbling. He got out of the water and thought about the beautiful ray that seemed happy to share its world with him.

Danny was deeply touched by this mystical experience. It was an enlightening moment and raised his awareness to the plight of the planet and its inhabitants. Danny will always remember the "ray with a face" and how it looked at him and "felt bad for us."

Creature Feature

The eagle spotted ray reaches a maximum wingspan of 10 feet, a mass of 500 pounds and a length, including the long tail, of 17 feet. This species is capable of leaping out of the water and sailing through the air when pursued. Its mouth contains two teeth-like plates used to crush shellfish, such as clams and oysters. The status of the spotted eagle ray is "near threatened," and the ray will qualify for "endangered" status in the near future if it continues to be over-fished.

Welcome To My Den

The famous marine scientist Jacques Cousteau proclaimed the spectacular coastal waters of British Columbia to be the best temperate diving in the world, and the second top spot after the tropical waters of the Red Sea. The area boasts the giant Pacific octopus, harbor seals, Stellar sea lions, sixgill sharks and killer whales. The lush kelp forests are home to a diverse number of fish, and rocky walls are a colorful garden of anemones, sea urchins and sponges.

Brent Cooke is a true nature lover and an avid photographer. He was living in Victoria amid world-class diving opportunities. He decided to learn to scuba dive in 1968 and was immediately addicted. His hobby quickly turned into a career, and in 1973, he started working in Marine Biology at the Royal British Columbia Museum in Victoria.

He explored thousands of dive sites along the coast and the surrounding islands, amassing an extensive underwater photographic collection of 14,000 marine life images over 12 years. Many of the photographs have won international awards and have been published in books.

Brent's job was to observe and photograph the animals in their natural habitat. Biologists were eager to improve their knowledge and understand the natural history of the ocean's inhabitants. Little was known about many of these creatures, and the diving community had labeled some of the more mysterious and intimidating species as dangerous.

One creature that earned a terrible reputation was the wolf-eel. A wolf-eel is not actually an eel; it is a large fish. The confusion is understandable— the wolf-eel has a long, slender, spotted body and swims by making S-shapes with its muscular body. A dorsal fin stretches from the head to the end of the body, which can grow to more than six feet in length.

But it's the face and not the body that has earned this fish a bad rap. The wolf-eel looks like a true sea monster, possessing a large head, a bulging forehead and oversized puffy lips. Its thick, power-ful jaws have sharp, wolf-like canines in front and pulverizing molars in the back. Even when its mouth is closed, its long, snaggly front teeth angle out, giving the fish a ferocious appearance.

The male's head is lighter in color than that of the female and is further distinguished by extra lumps and a set of big jowls, making him look like an old man. Truly, this creature has a face only a mother could love, and it is so hideously attrac-tive that you can't take your eyes off it.

The wolf-eel dines on hard-shelled, spiny sea urchins and crabs. It has muscles that strap under its lower jaw and wrap around the top of the skull, making it well equipped to crush and pulverize its prey. It is as foreboding in the fish world as the pit bull is in the dog world.

Brent remembers that in the late '60s, wolf-eels were regarded as "dastardly things," and any diver who ran across them was extremely apprehensive. "There was great fear of being attacked by wolf-eels, so we would stay back 10 feet from the hole and just look at their big, ugly head. Finally, we started to realize that even though they looked menacing, they never came charging out at us. In fact, they never did anything, just sat in their den."

This docile behavior did not match all the dreadful wolf-eel stories that floated through the scuba-diving community. As it turns out, wolf-eels are shy animals that like to hide; they stake out rock crevices and nooks to claim as their territory and reside in these dens for the duration of their lives.

For the next 20 years, as Brent continued to explore the underwater world, encountering many ominous and potentially dangerous animals in his travels, he continued to observe and photograph the wolf-eels from a guarded distance.

Then one day, Brent heard that someone had actually fed the frightening fish. Some daring diver had dropped a sea urchin in front of an occupied den. Sea urchins are one of the wolf-eel's favorite snacks, along with crab. The wolf-eel swam out to collect the tasty morsel and contentedly returned to its den.

That's all that happened: the wolf-eel picked up the sea urchin and swam back into his hole. The end.

Hardly fitting conduct for an animal whose reputation grew more sinister with each recounted story, making those who "lived to tell the tale" appear gutsy. One would think this fish was the next *Jaws*.

Because he had never seen any sign of aggression, Brent started to question the stories that surrounded this animal. One day in 1990, Brent was diving with a buddy in Saanich Inlet off Tyler Rock, northwest of Victoria. He was checking out the area when he noticed a wolf-eel snugly tucked in its rocky den. Brent took a large purple sea urchin, cut it in half with his dive knife and held out the palms of his hands, offering the delicacy to the wolf-eel.

"The wolf-eel eyed the sea urchin with interest and then looked at me. He swam out and, with the

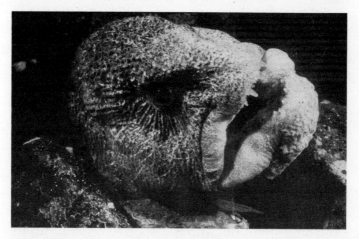

Captain Crunch, the wolf-eel, pokes his head out of his den to say hello.

gentlest of moves, took the urchin from my hands. It was a wonderful moment."

Brent was shocked by how calmly the fish approached him and the careful tenderness with which it plucked the urchin from his hands.

Brent could see from the big, bumpy head that this wolf-eel, stretching five feet in length, was an adult male. Inside the den lingered a female, her darker, smoother head poised at the opening. Wolf-eels are believed to mate for life, so it is common to find them in pairs.

Fascinated with this extraordinary encounter, Brent believed that wolf-eels had been falsely maligned. He decided he wanted to get to know them better and started to visit "Captain Crunch" and "Mrs. Crunch" on a regular basis.

On one dive, Brent beseeched his dive buddy to look past the wolf-eel's threatening veneer. He guaranteed his friend that Captain Crunch was friendly. After a little prodding and persuading, Brent convinced his pal to remove the diving regulator from his mouth, temporarily cutting off his air source, and replace it with a herring. Mrs. Crunch casually swam forward and carefully removed the herring from his mouth.

She seemed grateful for the treat and from then on would swim out into the open water column to greet Brent whenever he stopped by the den. Mrs. Crunch often pushed her way past the Captain to

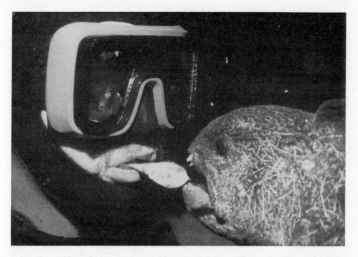

Mrs. Crunch takes a piece of herring from diver Gordon Green.

get at the food first. Then she would brush up to Brent and settle in for a "snuggle."

Over the next three years, Brent interacted with the two wolf-eels over and over again. "They acted like puppy dogs and would wind all over my body and wrap around my neck, arms and tank. It was incredible."

Brent reflects, "It was nice to see that their reputation was unfounded. This animal actually seemed trainable. The wolf-eel would see me and come right out to hang around with us. It is just incredible to interact with a wild animal in their environment, where they belong and we are the visitors. It is really neat to make that kind of connection. "

Fear of the wolf-eel had turned to fondness, proving that looks alone seldom tell the true story. Brent was happy to learn that this big, bad wolf-eel was really just a friendly ole sea puppy.

Something's Fishy!

Everyone loves a love story. But nothing beats the delight of reading about those unlikely, far-fetched pairings, such as Beauty and the Beast. We are told from the time we are tots that everybody deserves to be loved, so when mismatched affection finds a home, it's a great reason to shout "Hurray!"

Recently, photographs and a story entitled "Shark's Love" landed in my email inbox. My heart skipped a beat when I read the tale of a great white shark and a fisherman who had developed a mutual affection. Wow!

Imagine, one of the most feared creatures on Earth, a human-eating shark, forming a loving bond with a human. If Steven Spielberg had seen these photos, his famous film *Jaws* would have never become the first film to earn $100 million dollars at the box office. His 1975 blockbuster immortalized great whites around the world, branding them as merciless killing machines, not lovesick, overgrown minnows.

Jaws spread heart-pounding fear through the psyche of every swimmer and scuba diver on the planet. Every time I went for a dive, the soundtrack—Da-Dum, Da-Dum, Da-Dum—tripped through my head; I was spooked for a full year after seeing that film.

So the astonishing "love story" between Arnold Pointer, a professional fisherman in Australia, and a female great white shark named Cindy is a welcomed reprieve. It feels good to see these cunning predators through new eyes.

The story was first published in a French fishing magazine in 2006 and was nothing short of amazing. Arnold had come across the great white tangled in one of his fishing nets. The shark would have died had Arnold not gone to the trouble of setting her free. What he didn't expect was that the grateful 17-foot-long shark would start to follow him wherever he went. Now, a great white can reach 21 feet in length and weigh up to 4800 pounds, so I can imagine that having this big fish trail behind your boat like a puppy would be a bit unnerving.

The French magazine, *Le Magazine des Voyages de Pêche*, printed Arnold's concerns: "It's been two years and she doesn't leave me alone. She follows me everywhere I go, and her presence scares all the fishes. I don't know what to do anymore."

But as the story unfolds, we learn that Arnold has grown fond of Cindy as well. "Once I stop the boat, she comes to me, she turns on her back and lets me pet her belly and neck, she grunts, turns her eyes and moves her fins up and down hitting the water happily...."

The photos are compelling and support the tale. The opening photo shows a man in a small sea kayak looking over his shoulder at an enormous torpedo-shaped fish cutting through the water behind him. I have to say, the kayak looks absolutely puny beside the shark.

A series of other spectacular photos show a man patting the side of the shark's head, her mouth wide open and rows of triangular, serrated, razor-sharp teeth, each about three inches long, gleaming brightly. There is even a photo in which the man stretches out his arm as the shark surfaces and gently touches her pointed nose as if the beast was a trained guppy.

It is all so contrary to the stories we've heard about this maniacal, vengeful, bloodthirsty species. This love story is too good to be true. And, as it turns out, it is *not* true.

The French magazine published the article as an April Fool's Day prank. The story was later translated from French to English and hit the Internet with full steam. What makes the story so easy to believe is the collection of images. The photos are stunning and are totally authentic; they have just been taken out of context.

A pair of marine biologists and shark experts, Michael C. Scholl and Thomas P. Peschak took the images during their field research. The photos depict several sharks, not just the lovesick "Cindy." The photos do show a man touching the shark, but it was part of his research and in no way communicates the finned creature's appreciation or affection for the human. Sadly, sharks are biologically incapable of being bitten by the "love bug" and cannot express such emotions. The biologists' research revealed that when they rested a hand on the shark's nose, the eyes would remain open. But, if they slid their hand closer to the eyes, the shark would roll them back to protect them. They discovered that the eyes rolling back was not in response to the shark opening its mouth as previously believed, but rather an action to protect the eyes.

So there you have it, the wild and wonderful hoax I promised you in Chapter Seven. Too bad, I say, because "Shark's Love" was a terrific love story. *And* it had pretty much erased my fears of accidentally bumping into *Jaws* while diving in the tropics. Da-Dum, Da-Dum, Da-Dum....

Creature Feature

Great white sharks have been around for approximately 409 million years. They are the largest predatory fish on Earth and can have up to 3000 teeth at one time. Shark attacks are quite rare, and few species are considered dangerous to humans. Each year, more people are bitten by dogs than by sharks. Bees kill 20 times more people per year in the U.S. alone than sharks kill worldwide.

NOTES ON SOURCES

Books

Baumgartl, Nomi and Chris Gallucci. *Elephant Man*. Richmond Hill: Firefly Books, 2008.

Berman, Ruth and Cheryl Walsh Bellville. *American Bison*. Minneapolis: Carolrhoda Books, 1992.

Bonner, Jeffrey P. *Sailing With Noah*. Columbia: University of Missouri Press, 2006.

Dodd, Johnny. "Bella and Tarra." *People*. Vol. 71, No. 17. May 4, 2009.

Eiseley, Loren. *The Star Thrower*. Boston: Houghton Mifflin Harcourt, 1979.

Goodall, Jane. "Chimpanzees—Bridging the Gap." In *The Great Ape Project: Equality Beyond Humanity*. Eds. Paola Cavalieri and Peter Singer. New York: St. Martin's Griffin, 1993.

Hatkoff, Isabella, Craig Hatkoff and Paula Kahumbu. *Owen & Mzee: The Language of Friendship*. New York: Scholastic Press, 2007.

Pepperberg, Irene. *Alex & Me*. New York: HarperCollins, 2008.

Websites

Many websites were visited in the research and writing of this book. Here is a list of the key sites:

ABC Radio National, The Science Show
alaskas-spirit.com
Alberta.ca (Fish and Wildlife)
alexfoundation.org

animal-rights-library.com
archive.deseretnews.com
Associated Press
baileythebuffalo.com
BBC
Canadian Eskimo Dog Foundation
CBS News
chrisgallucci-theelephantman.com
CNN
Con Slobodchikoff
Daily Dachshund and Dog News
Daily Mail
Edmonton Journal
Edmonton Valley Zoo
habitatharmony.org
Hoax-Slayer
International Shark Attack Research Fund
Karvonen Films
KOMO News
luluthekangaroo.com
members.shaw.ca/neweyesforroxy/index.htm
Miracle Pets
National Geographic News
National Institute for Play
National Public Radio
NBC
New York Times
Norbert Rosing
Nuneaton Warwickshire Wildlife Sanctuary
owenandmzee.com (Stephen Tuei's Caretaker Blog)
Pet Rescue Magazine: petrescuemagazine.com
polarbearworld.com
prairiedogcoalition.org
purina.ca
Safari Zoological Park
sanjose.bizjournals.com

Sea-Star Aquarium
Seattle Times
Second Chance Animal Rescue Society: scarscare.org
shambala.org
Snopes
spca.bc.ca
St. Louis Post Post-Dispatch
surfline.com
The Canadian Press, Canwest News Service
The Daily News
The Daily Telegraph
The Early Show
The Elephant Sanctuary
The Gorilla Foundation: Koko.org
The Responsible Animal Care Society: tracs-bc.ca
The Telegraph
Today Show
Wildlife Rehabilitation Society of Edmonton: wildlife-
    edm.ca